The Real Price of War

"Worth Paying For," by Edwin Marcus. Copyright 1941.

THE REAL PRICE OF WAR

How You Pay for the War on Terror

Joshua S. Goldstein

New York University Press

New York and London

NEW YORK UNIVERSITY PRESS
New York and London
www.nyupress.org

Frontispiece: "Worth Paying For," by Edwin Marcus.
Copyright 1941.
Library of Congress reproduction number 2a10522.
Reprinted by permission of Donald E. Marcus, whom I thank.

Library of Congress Cataloging-in-Publication Data
Goldstein, Joshua S., 1952–
The real price of war : how you pay for the war on terror /
Joshua S. Goldstein.
p. cm.
Includes bibliographical references and index.
ISBN 0–8147–3161–9 (cloth : alk. paper)
1. War on Terrorism, 2001—Economic aspects.
2. Terrorism—Prevention—Economic aspects—United States.
3. War—Economic aspects—United States.
4. Government spending policy—United States.   I. Title.
HV6432.G64   2004
973.931—dc22   2004008513

New York University Press books are printed on acid-free paper,
and their binding materials are chosen for strength and durability.

Manufactured in the United States of America

10 9 8 7 6 5 4 3 2 1

CONTENTS

PREFACE

Although it focuses on the American economy in wartime, this is not an economics book. As a political scientist and interdisciplinary scholar of war, I see the economy as just one of various arenas in which the effects of war play out. In this book, I trace the costs and economic effects of the War on Terror, broadly defined. I sketch the big picture of war funding—the dollars that come from your pocket and ultimately pay for war-related needs. Then I show how the economic stresses of war play out far beyond government budgets, with the conclusion that being at war exacts a high economic cost—higher the longer the war goes on. Finally, I question whether we are spending enough on the War on Terror to have a reasonable chance to end it quickly, which means that future costs will be higher and harder to meet. The book's three parts reflect three layers of war costs: first, the money we spend through our government; second, the private and indirect costs to our economy; and third, the additional costs we may need to pay in the coming years.

My aim is both to inform and to provoke debate. I hope to raise questions, to draw attention to underdiscussed issues, and to help roll back denial about the War on Terror and its costs. I doubt anyone will agree with all of this book, but I hope everyone finds some part of it thought-provoking.

I find fault with the administration and Congress during the first two years of the War on Terror for both conservative and liberal reasons. Liberal readers may welcome my criticisms of President Bush and my demonstration of how the high costs of being at war fall on Americans. But those readers may find less comfortable my argument that by spending even more on the War on Terror we could *win* the war sooner, avoiding a decades-long fight and perhaps saving our cities from destruction. President Bush has not adequately funded the war in all its dimensions—because war funding competes directly with tax cuts—nor has he mobilized and united the country for the effort. If we are to defeat global terrorism, I argue, we need to muster more resources on each of three fronts: the military, homeland security, and foreign aid/diplomacy. Ending the war—and what end can there be but winning?—would create conditions for a more stable and peaceful world order in which our economy could prosper again. I'm not *sure* that victory over all terrorist groups of global reach is possible, but it *might* be possible, and if so I'm pretty sure it will need more money. Our best strategy, in my view, is to spend what it takes now to get the job done. It won't be cheaper in future years. And the way to raise that money, clearly, is to increase wealthy Americans' taxes, among other less important revenue sources.

The numbers in the book are rounded off and presented on the scale of a household's monthly expenditures rather than in the billions of dollars discussed in national policy debates. This helps create an understandable big picture of war's place in the federal government and the overall economy, although at the cost of economic precision.

In summarizing the federal government's finances, I put off to one side the retirement system, in which payroll taxes fund Social Security, Medicare, and the federal retirement system. This makes my analysis of the deficit more alarming than the official "unified" budget—alarming enough on its own—which counts $200 billion a year in retirement surpluses as though they were reductions in current deficits.

In creating a mosaic of life in wartime America, I relied heavily on journalists' accounts in local newspapers across the country—accessible to all of us these days via Google News on the Internet. Where I have omitted page numbers it is generally because the story appeared on the publication's Web site without a page number. I draw especially on the *New York Times* as the nation's "newspaper of record" and the voice of New York City, which is the central front in the war at home.

A Web site about the book—www.realpriceofwar.com— includes further information and a discussion forum.

—Joshua S. Goldstein
Amherst, Massachusetts
February 2004

INTRODUCTION

The first ambulance that arrived at Overlake Hospital Medical Center in Bellevue, Washington, carried a young woman named Vivian Chamberlain, screaming in pain and bleeding from her punctured eardrums. When handheld radiation detectors went wild, she was stripped of her outer clothing, brushed down by four workers in protective suits, and hosed off with cold hydrant water. More ambulances followed, as waves of similar casualties hit Seattle-area hospitals. This was only a test, part of a simulation in 2003 to improve America's ability to respond to a terrorist "dirty bomb" or a biological weapon. But, as the volunteer-victim Chamberlain told the *Seattle Times*, "it was real-life scary."[1]

Also real-life scary were the economic realities at the company where Chamberlain worked, Boeing. The War on Terror has cost Boeing, its workers, and its business partners dearly. The company laid off thousands of workers in 2003, pushing Boeing job losses since 9/11 above thirty-five thousand. Boeing's CEO Phil Condit called it "the worst downturn since airplanes existed." As an economist for the state Department of Employment Security put it, "Everybody knows somebody who's been laid off from Boeing."[2] With people traveling less since the 9/11 terrorist attacks, airlines going bankrupt, and a fleet of jets sitting idle in the California desert, there was little hope of a quick turnaround in Boeing's fortunes. The troubles of Boeing, long a mainstay of the Seattle economy and the aerospace industry, reverberated widely.

The economic costs of this war are not incidental. Terrorists are targeting our economy and trying to make the war as expensive as possible. This is a war of attrition designed to weaken America. Listen to Osama bin Laden, in a videotape three months after 9/11: America may not be beatable militarily, he said—Al Qaeda had just lost its last major Afghan sanctuary in Tora Bora—but "there is another way through hitting the economic structure. . . . It is very important to concentrate on hitting the U.S. economy through all possible means."[3] Al Qaeda and similar groups could inflict serious economic harm just by keeping the war going year after year, because it is both expensive and disruptive of economic life.

As Vivian Chamberlain returned to work at Boeing, the terror drill over for her, thousands of desperately ill patients flooded into hospitals in Chicago and were quickly diagnosed with pneumonic plague from a terrorist biological weapon. In the suburb of Skokie, triage tents were set up outside Rush North Shore Medical Center, just one of 157 hospitals responding. The hospital's trauma coordinator, Barbara Croak, said, "We're in full code triage, full disaster mode."[4] It was another phase of the exercise, of course. The majority of victims were just faxed in to local hospitals rather than showing up in person. In a real attack, they would need rides in the ambulances of the Skokie Fire Department, which would also provide paramedic and rescue services, hazardous materials response, and disaster management. But "first responders" like the Skokie Fire Department and similar agencies across the Chicago area depend on local funding, which has been tight. As the hospitals filled with fax-victims in 2003, the drug company Pfizer was closing up shop in Skokie for good, taking with it fifteen hundred Chicago-area jobs and $5 million a year in property taxes that Pfizer used to pay. Those property taxes used to help fund, among other things, the Skokie Fire Department.

America's challenges on two fronts—war and the economy—are intimately linked, just as Seattle and Chicago residents practice for civil defense while looking over their shoulders nervously at layoffs and service cuts. Job losses in Seattle and Chicago reflected a broader malaise that settled across the American economy during the first two years of the War on Terror. The uncertainties of wartime deepened the economic slowdown of 2001 to early 2003. The worst job market in a generation—two million jobs lost in two years—accompanied a succession of corporate bankruptcies, from Enron to WorldCom to United Airlines. The dollar dropped in value. World oil prices, a key economic variable, whipped up and down with the shifting risks related to war and terror—an instability that undercut growth. Spiraling federal deficits also reduced confidence, and budget shortfalls forced cutbacks in safety-net programs. The increased military spending and the costs of homeland security have piled hundreds of billions of dollars onto the federal deficit. The war did not create the economic downswing in 2001–3, which began officially in the first quarter of 2001 after the dotcom collapse. But the war added to it.

Economic growth roared back in late 2003, heading into election year (that's how politicians plan it), but two huge problems remained. First, the rapidly escalating U.S. budget deficits—partly the result of war spending, partly of historically unprecedented wartime tax cuts, among other factors—could weaken the economy (by lowering the dollar's value and raising interest rates and prices). Second, another terrorist attack on U.S. soil could disrupt economic life in ways yet unknown. Historically, in wartime, people consume less and businesses hold off on investment because of risks and anxieties. Future terrorist attacks could create a chronic anxiety that would unsettle the economy, the equivalent of a low-grade fever. Worse still, our enemies seek nuclear weapons to destroy our cities. The economic effects of such future terrorist attacks could be catastrophic. Meanwhile, international trade—an engine of prosperity in the 1990s—would suffer if America closed its borders in a prolonged period of danger.

Letting the War on Terror drag on for decades would be the most costly option. Yet that's just where we seem to be heading. In its early years, the war consumed enough money to drive up the federal deficit to breathtaking heights, yet—as I show in the later chapters of this book—not enough money to really get the job done on any of several "fronts." I conclude that our best chance for peace and prosperity requires more economic sacrifices in the short term as we pursue the war in all its aspects with greater vigor. Because of his commitment to tax cuts, President George W. Bush shortchanged the war effort, especially its nonmilitary components, and failed to mobilize the country behind it.

These truths should be self-evident: The nation is at war. The war is expensive. Someone has to pay for it. The sooner we honestly assess the costs and divide them fairly among ourselves, the sooner we can mobilize the country's full resources for the war. The price is not beyond reach; it will take a smaller fraction of the national economy than past wars have claimed. We will have to dig deep in our pockets, but in the end we can afford the price of this war. What we cannot afford is to stay in denial about the real price of war. You may disagree with the policies and methods by which the Bush administration has fought this war, such as its Iraq campaign, but we must fight the overall war. We are not going to solve the problem on the cheap, and we cannot afford to count on getting lucky.

In this war, not to win is to lose. The Bush administration compiled, in the first two years after 9/11, a perfect record of zero attacks against the U.S. homeland. The trouble is, there's zero—meaning the danger is gone, we have removed the threat—and then there's zero meaning it hasn't happened yet. We cannot be content with the second kind of zero. Even if we reduced the odds of a nuclear attack by chasing after terrorists, disrupting their finances, arresting some leaders, and breaking up some cells, those odds might not be good enough. Imagine, for instance, that we reduced the chances of a catastrophic attack on any given day to one-hundredth of 1 percent. If rain had odds like that, you wouldn't take an umbrella. But those odds would look less appealing if the war drags on without end. The chance of a catastrophic attack within thirty years would be 80 percent. Nuclear terrorism is not like rain, something we learn to live with; nuclear terrorism is like rain to the Wicked Witch of the West, something that can melt us.

Preventing the destruction of our cities must be the central purpose of the War on Terror and, indeed, of the nation itself. In this sense, President Bush's rhetoric about the nature of the war is not too expansive. He thinks of the War on Terror as a unified effort that will continue for years and span many "fronts" and countries. Afghanistan and Iraq were just "battles," to use Bush's term. Worldwide in scope, open-ended in time, the War on Terror is at once a desperate struggle to save American cities from destruction and an ambitious mission extending to "every dark corner of the earth" (again Bush's phrase, in 2003).[5] Bush may be wrong about the mix of military and nonmilitary means, about how and why he fights military campaigns, and about having God on his side in fighting "evil," but the war itself matters as much as he says it does. This expansive view of the scope of the war cannot, however, coexist with a long-duration war that lasts for generations. Rather, we must end the war in years, not decades.

Ending the war means winning the war. Given the nature of Al Qaeda and related groups, the only end for the war is to put out of business all such terrorist organizations of global reach. Is this a big job? Yes. Is it impossible? No. Few terrorists have global reach, and few of those have the resources and popular base of Al Qaeda and its network of affiliated groups worldwide. The Iraq war aside, the hunt for terrorists has the support of virtually all the world's governments and the legitimacy of UN backing. The United States, most powerful country in the history of the world, the country that won World War II in less than four years, can defeat Al Qaeda and its affiliates.

As I discuss toward the end of the book, I think this effort will require much more than military means. In some ways, we need to remake the world and America's place in it. So when I speak of the "war," I do not mean only, or even primarily, military campaigns.

How to win the War on Terror is not the subject of this book. How to pay for it is. Both questions are politically contentious, but they are not the same question. Whatever disagreements about strategy Americans may have, any successful strategy will be expensive. The problem of paying for the war will be with us in the coming years, no matter who occupies the Oval Office. The president in 2005 will have on his plate an unfinished job in Afghanistan, ongoing attacks in Iraq, vast backlogged needs in homeland security, a tide of anti-Americanism worldwide, and U.S. conflicts with major allies who must help us if we are to defeat terrorism. None of it will be cheap to solve.

Raising needed resources for the War on Terror is politically problematic because it is a distributional issue on which the interests of Americans diverge. Seemingly, nobody wants to pay more than their share, and the politics of government spending dictate that an undue burden will fall on those either too weak to protect their interests or patriotic enough to shoulder a heavy load voluntarily. For instance, the National Guard and reservists discussed at the end of Chapter 7 sacrifice by risking harm and being separated from their families, but they also take huge financial losses in going from civilian to military pay for extended periods. Congress could more equitably distribute the burden of war by making up these pay reductions and passing on the bill to all of us in the form of slightly higher taxes. Or it could force companies to make up their reservist employees' lost pay, as a few companies such as IBM already do. But raising taxes and loading regulations on companies are politically unpopular proposals, especially for Republicans.

The political difficulties around paying for the War on Terror in its first few years left the fight against terrorism with inadequate resources on all its fronts—from distant regime change, to homeland security, to the battle for worldwide public opinion. Given the high price of war, the high price of failure, and the political difficulties of getting Americans to pay more taxes, one can understand why politicians would rather not face up. But denial is no substitute for policy.

The Real Price of War makes three central arguments. First, the war is more expensive than you thought, especially if you include hidden, indirect, and future costs. Second, we have little choice but to pay the price, and probably a rising price, in the coming years. Third, President Bush and the Congress have not been honest with the public about the real price of this war, which competes with tax cuts and other political priorities, so we still need a debate about how we split the bill for war. Liberal readers will need to consider the possibility that the war deserves even more money and attention than President Bush has given it; conservative readers will need to consider the possibility that we need to raise taxes to pay for the war.

Part One

GOVERNMENT SPENDING

War . . . has but one thing certain, and that is to increase taxes.

—Thomas Paine, 1787

Chapter One

WHAT DOES WAR COST?

Imagine the costs of war as a series of boxes nested inside each other (Box 1). The innermost box is U.S. costs in Iraq, which received growing public attention in 2003 as postwar security and reconstruction costs mounted. But Iraq is just, as President Bush says, a "battle." It is contained in a much larger box, the War on Terror, which also contains military operations in Afghanistan, worldwide counterterrorism efforts, CIA covert actions, homeland security, and possibly future wars in places like Iran or North Korea. In turn, the War on Terror is nested in a much larger box that I call "U.S. government war-related spending." In addition to the War on Terror, this war-related spending includes "peacetime" military forces—baseline costs to maintain standing military forces—as well as veterans' benefits and the interest on past war debts.

Box 1 Nested costs of war.

Iraq (liberation, occupation, reconstruction)

Afghanistan
CIA and other counterterrorism
Homeland security
Future wars?

The War on Terror

Peacetime" military forces, salaries, facilities
Training, equipment, supplies
Veterans' benefits
Interest on past war debts

U.S. Government War-Related Spending

Destruction of capital in war zones (e.g., New York)
Additional costs to business and local government
   in wartime
Effects of rising national debt
Compounding of budget shortfalls
War-induced inflation

The Real Price of War

The even larger box within which the government's war-related spending is nested I call the "real price of war." It includes—in addition to the government's war-related spending—the disruption and destruction caused by wartime, the growing national debt, indirect impacts on state and local governments, and inflation, the ultimate war tax throughout history. I turn to these indirect costs in Part 2 of the book.

The first chapters, however, focus on the government's war-related spending. Among the many ways in which war and the economy affect each other, the most important is simply that being at war costs a lot of money—money that ultimately must come from the pocketbooks of Americans. War expenditures go far beyond the costs of fighting in particular places, such as Iraq. We have to pay for both active fighting and the broader maintenance of standing military forces. War is not an event that comes and goes but an ongoing process that ebbs and flows over the years. "Wartime" is a more active, and more expensive, phase of that process.

The Parking Meter in Your Living Room

To see what the U.S. government's war-related spending costs your household, let's install a parking meter in your living room. Put a quarter in the meter and you get twenty minutes of security against foreign threats to our country; six quarters gets you two hours. Keep feeding the meter around the clock, 24/7, year-round. That's what war spending costs the average U.S. household.

The quarters that go into the parking meter probably will not bankrupt your household. And military spending does not dominate the economy either. But it's not trivial. The quarters add up to about $500 per month. That puts military spending up there with the big monthly bills—less than the mortgage, more than the phone bill. If you saved this amount every month for eighteen years, you could send your kid to a good private college.

We can compute the bill for *your* household rather than the *average* U.S. household. The $500-a-month bill is for a household income on the order of $50,000 to $100,000 (depending on household size and circumstances). If your household income is somewhat above $100,000, you pay double the average (and more for still higher incomes), so your household bill for war-related spending is $1,000 a month or more. If your income is just below $50,000, you pay about half (and less still for lower incomes), so your household bill is $250 a month or less. Obviously, individual cases vary, but these are the magnitudes of money the government raises for war. (About half comes from income taxes, and most of the rest is borrowed.)

Thinking about Large Numbers

I express money in terms of costs per average household because of the problem of scale in thinking about military spending and other costs of war. We are not used to thinking about very large numbers—millions, billions, trillions. Johnny Carson made fun of the late astronomer Carl Sagan, describing the number of stars in the universe as "billions and billions," but the actual number is on the order of magnitude of ten *trillion* billions. It is hard to get our minds around numbers on these large scales. And so it is with military budgets and budget deficits, each of which total hundreds of billions of dollars a year. If you are an American citizen who understands where these vast sums come from and go to, you are the exception.

To help translate the blur of large-scale budgets into the language of everyday life, take a $10 bill out of your wallet. That $10 bill is to your household what $1 billion is to the whole country. (There are about one hundred million households in the country; $10 for each household makes $1 billion.) So, for example, when Congress approved a nearly $80 billion supplemental appropriation in March 2003 to pay for the war in Iraq and related costs, your household's share of that was eighty

$10 bills, or $800. And your share of the next such appropriation in October 2003, $87 billion, was about $870 more. (Again, if your household income is somewhat above $100,000, pay double; if slightly below $50,000, pay half.)

As the economist John Maynard Keynes said, it is better to be "vaguely right than precisely wrong."[1] To get the big picture of war and the economy, we need to think in orders of magnitude—powers of ten—and be only "vaguely right" about the specific numbers. Throughout this book I round off numbers to try to make the big picture understandable.

Where the Money Goes

Using the $10 bill trick, you can see that the $500 a month the average household pays for external security is fifty $10 bills, which translates to $50 billion a month for the whole country. That's $600 billion per year. This is an approximation, and in fact there is no exact total because it depends on definitions and judgments. But the overview is in Box 2.[2] The regular defense budget itself, since a sharp post-9/11 increase, stands at $400 billion a year, or more than $300 a month per household. Of this, 95 percent is for the Department of Defense, with 5 percent for the nuclear weapons responsibilities of the Department of Energy. "The Pentagon," then, is the main claim on your household's contributions to the national defense.

Pentagon expenses are themselves multilayered. Specific campaigns such as Iraq and Afghanistan—and potentially others—come and go side by side with an ongoing, worldwide effort to destroy Al Qaeda and other nonstate terrorist groups. All these and other military operations are overlaid on the routine maintenance of the world's preeminent military forces—costs like salaries, training, and weapons procurement. These

Box 2 The bill for war-related spending
per average household monthly.

UNITED STATES GOVERNMENT
WASHINGTON, D.C.

The Smith Household
12345 Main St.
Anytown, USA

Amount due for war-related services rendered this month.

Your contract plan includes the following services:

Defense Department	$300 per month
Energy Department for nuclear weapons	15
Homeland Security	25
Other agencies	10
Veterans Affairs	50
Servicing Past Military Debt	40
Iraq War	60
Total	**$500**

Note: Half of this total has been deducted from your paycheck this
month. Currently your plan calls for borrowing most of the rest
through the National Debt Credit Card Company. Please let us
know if you wish to change plans in the future.

"peacetime" costs are a necessary price of admission—our
forces must be trained, weapons developed, and bases main-
tained—before military operations can occur. New types of
spending in the post-9/11 wartime period add on more costs.

But the Pentagon is only two-thirds of the government's
military-related spending. For one thing, the costs of homeland
security outside the Defense Department add to the costs of
wartime since 9/11. They come to more than $30 billion annu-

ally—$25 a month per household. Of that, more than two-thirds goes to the new Department of Homeland Security, with the rest spread throughout the federal government, especially the Departments of Health and Human Services, Justice, and Energy. Furthermore, various government agencies also perform national security functions that are not included in the Pentagon or Homeland Security Department budgets. For instance, the CIA plays a key role in the War on Terror and is not part of the Pentagon budget. And NASA provides infrastructure used extensively by military satellites. These agencies' contributions to national security cost on the order of $10 a month per household.

The salaries of the soldiers fighting our wars are included in the Pentagon budget. But veterans' benefits are not. Those benefits supplement the fairly low salaries of soldiers and are an inducement for enlistment in the all-volunteer military. They are a cost of war, even though payment is delayed. So add them to the tab: $50 per month per household.

Now comes money we are paying out currently as interest on past military debts. We have sharply increased the national debt to fund military spending on various historical occasions, most recently during the Reagan-era military buildup of the 1980s, in the last decade of the Cold War. We are doing it again, spectacularly, in the current war. It is hard to estimate how much of the accumulated debt is due to military spending. (Borrowed money goes into a big pot with other government funds and is spent for a range of government activities.) Antiwar organizations give various estimates, finding from one hundred billion to several hundred billion dollars a year in interest payments to be due to earlier military spending.[3] To be conservative about this controversial item, let's put it at half of the low end of this range: $50 billion per year. That works out for the average household to $40 per month. It is a number that will increase dramatically in the next few years of ballooning federal deficits.

Finally, the war in Iraq was not included in the regular budget just discussed. Congress appropriated nearly $80 billion extra, mostly for Iraq-related operations, in the last half of the 2003 fiscal year, and $87 billion more for fiscal year 2004. (The government's fiscal year starts in October of the previous year.) In mid-2003, the Pentagon estimated that ongoing postwar operations in Iraq, narrowly defined, were costing $5 billion per month—nearly $50 per household. But with attacks on U.S. forces in Iraq increasing in late 2003, this number appeared likely to grow. The $87 billion supplemental appropriation for fiscal 2004, which included some non-Iraq expenses, came to nearly $70 per household per month. So we can take $60 per month per household as a pretty good approximation of the ongoing costs of U.S. activities in Iraq. Whether you think invading Iraq was a necessary part of the War on Terror or a mistake, we are there now and can't quickly cut these costs.

That's how your household's $500 monthly bill for government war-related spending adds up. Now you'd better take that billion-dollar $10 bill out of your wallet again, to feed tonight's parking meter. Park yourself on the couch, and don't get too far from the meter. It will need another billion-dollar bill in about fourteen hours.

Costs of Terrorist Attacks

A new kind of cost in this war is the damage to U.S. lives and property from terrorist attacks. The government will pay at least some of these costs. The damage to property and the economic losses from deaths and injuries in the 9/11 attack are hard to estimate in dollar terms. Most estimates range from tens of billions of dollars to more than $100 billion all told, depending on assumptions and methods.

The U.S. government has gotten into some trouble trying to estimate the value of lives lost on 9/11. It started with what seemed like a simple political idea, passed into law by Congress—that families of 9/11 victims would be compensated financially by the government. This would spread some of the burden of that trauma across all taxpayers instead of it being borne solely by bereaved families of those unlucky enough—or in some cases heroic enough—to have died in the attacks that day. But the hastily passed legislation specified not just a payment for each victim but payments designed to compensate for families' financial losses from a death. The fund's administrator, Kenneth Feinberg, had to develop complex formulas to determine what each person's earning power was and the number of years left in their working life, then deduct life insurance benefits and so forth. It turned out that rich families got much higher payments—multimillion-dollar payments in quite a few cases—than did poor families. "If somebody is earning $1 million a year," Feinberg asks, and the formulas dictate a payment of $10 million, "should the taxpayer and this program subsidize a $10 million lifestyle and a $10 million tax-free award? Should 15 percent of the people get 85 percent of the money? That isn't what Congress intended. If Congress had thought this through for more than a few hours, I don't believe that's what they would have said."[4]

An additional problem was that some families of victims of earlier Al Qaeda attacks—notably the bombing of the U.S. embassies in Kenya and Tanzania and the USS *Cole*—as well as victims of the Oklahoma City bombing, felt that the government seemed to downgrade the value of their loved ones' lives by compensating only the 9/11 victims while leaving them on their own.

There were also some hard feelings among spouses of soldiers killed in Iraq and Afghanistan, who received a $6,000
"death gratuity" plus about $1,000 to $1,500 a month until re-
marriage, and usually life insurance payments. Kelly Gibbons,
whose husband died in Afghanistan early in 2003, told
Newsweek she completely sympathized with 9/11 victims'
families, but "these people who never even thought to put their
lives on the line for anybody else are getting millions of dollars." Gibbons's own survivor benefits, $1,422 a month, barely
covered the mortgage.[5] In mid-2003, Congress passed legislation to increase a range of military benefits, and to extend others where they were scheduled to expire. These include doubling the death gratuity to $12,000 retroactively, extending
"hostile fire/imminent danger" pay and family separation allowances, and making more pay and benefits tax-free. But society still doesn't compensate financially for soldiers' sacrifices.

The 9/11 victim compensation fund illustrates both the high
economic costs incurred by the deaths of Americans and the
rarity of anyone compensating those costs. Usually they are
borne primarily by the survivors, the children, the companies
where people had worked, and the communities where they
lived. The deaths of Americans in the course of this war—at
home and abroad, civilian and military—are economic costs, although of course much more than that. The economic costs
generally are not counted, not charged to the government, and
not included in what you pay for war at the parking meter in
your living room. In the rare case, 9/11, in which government
has tried to estimate and compensate for the economic losses,
they turned out to be quite large indeed.

Future Attacks

An additional cost of this war—though impossible to measure ahead of time—is the damage that would be inflicted by future terrorist attacks on the United States. U.S. government policy is based on the assumption that future attacks probably will occur despite efforts being made to prevent them. Costs would depend on the type of attack. The effects of weapons of mass destruction would be far more expensive than, say, shooting down an airplane or bombing a resort. In the worst case, this war could see the destruction of one or more U.S. cities by nuclear bombs.

Insurance premiums reflect the best thinking by experts about the risks and costs of future events. Businesses facing possible losses from future terrorist attacks have turned to insurance companies for protection. But after 9/11, when direct losses were estimated around $40 billion, insurance companies withdrew coverage for terrorist attacks. The companies that provided any terrorism insurance in 2002 did so at very high premiums. This put potential target cities, especially New York, at a disadvantage in terms of businesses locating there, as Senator Charles Schumer explained: "Many in New York can't get terrorism insurance and those who can have been put at an extreme disadvantage because it's so expensive. This has basically hurt New York and other cities more than other places." In late 2002, Congress stepped in to guarantee insurance against terrorist attacks. The new law requires all commercial insurers to offer terrorism coverage and, after a few years of phase-in, to pay up to 15 percent of their premiums toward damages. The government will pay 90 percent of damages above $15 billion, up to $100 billion a year for the first three years.[6] So the bottom line is that future terrorist attacks will ultimately be added to your bill for government war-related spending.

Negative Economics

The entire cost-benefit analysis of the War on Terror, and of war in general, rests on a negative kind of economics. The "benefits" consist of a reduction in losses. We incur the costs of military forces and operations in order to reduce the losses from terrorist attacks or other external threats. The situation resembles the choice you face if an armed robber demands your wallet. Giving up the wallet to save your life is clearly preferable. But if there is no check on armed robbers, eventually you will be accosted by them daily. So you will either buy weapons to defend yourself, or pay taxes to support a police force to protect you, or both. Either could be a worthwhile expenditure, if used well to prevent even higher costs, but they are still costs. And the same is true of a national defense budget. Losing a wallet or a city, paying for a gun or an army, training police or testing homeland security capabilities, all incur costs without generating wealth. There are exceptions, but this is the rule: war is an economic negative.

To recap, about $500 per month is what the government spends, per household, on war-related budgets, including veterans' benefits and homeland security expenses. About a third of this is the increase since 9/11. It will not bankrupt us, but it is a substantial cost. The next three chapters consider where this money comes from.

Chapter Two

TAXES

Line 54 on your 2003 federal income tax Form 1040 does not even have a name. Officially it is called "Subtract line 53 from line 43. If line 53 is more than line 43, enter -0-." But line 54 is important. It is your total income tax bill for the year. (If you use Form 1040EZ, it's line 10; on Form 1040A, it's line 38.) The rest of Form 1040, after line 54, adds on payroll and self-employment taxes that pay for Social Security and Medicare. But the income tax part, on line 54, is where you pay for war. (I am going to put both the payroll taxes and the payouts made under Social Security and Medicare to one side.)

In fact, you can take one-third of line 54 to get a fair approximation of your income tax payments for war-related spending.[1] (These income tax payments cover about half the war-related spending, the rest being mostly borrowed.) The average income tax paid by a U.S. household is about $700 a month. So about a third of that, under $250 a month, pays for war. That payment, plus the war spending financed by debt and by other revenue sources, adds up to the $500-a-month "parking meter in your living room" described in Chapter 1. The other two-thirds of your line 54 go to keep the rest of the federal government running, including all the federal programs and agencies unrelated to war (but not Social Security and Medicare).

You get to the number on line 54 through the Tax Tables, which show how your adjusted, deducted income translates into your tax due. The Tax Tables reflect overall tax rates by which certain income brackets are taxed at certain rates.

The income tax is a "progressive" tax, meaning that rich people pay a larger proportion of their income than do poor people. This means that upper-income Americans pay the most, proportionately, to fund war-related spending. Poor Americans have long fought our wars while rich Americans paid for them. How progressive the tax rates should be—what actual rates should apply to what incomes—is a matter for the U.S. Congress.

Box 3 on page 26 shows how different income brackets contribute to the total income tax collected.[2] Clearly, upper-middle-class and rich Americans provide most of the money that pays for war and other federal expenses. Indeed, the top 10 percent of taxpayers account for more than half the money collected. (Again, I am putting to one side the payroll taxes that fund Social Security and Medicare. Those taxes take a larger share of income from poor Americans than from rich ones.)

Historically, in and after wartime, tax rates have both increased and become more progressive—that is, increasing more for the rich than for the poor. In the Civil War, the economic strengths of the North were a major factor in the outcome, and the ability to tax successfully was one of those strengths. The

Confederacy could cover only about 5 percent of its expenses with tax revenues, while the Union covered 20 percent, reports economic history writer John Steele Gordon. The newly created forerunner of today's Internal Revenue Service (IRS) "levied taxes on nearly everything": excise taxes, stamp taxes, tolls, tariffs, and a first-ever tax on all income (whose top bracket peaked at 10 percent in 1864). People did not evade the new taxes, according to Gordon. "One of the natural principles of taxation, it turns out, is that people willingly pay very high taxes during wartime."[3] It is a principle that today's politicians could study.

Looking just at the top tax bracket—defined in most historical periods as taxable income above about $200,000 to $400,000—the tax rate on these very-high-income Americans has risen sharply during and after each major war. During World War I the top tax rate jumped from below 10 percent before 1916 to about 70 percent in 1917–21. The 70 percent rate kicked in for income above $1 million. During World War II the top tax rate rose from 81 percent in 1941 (on income above $5 million) to 94 percent in 1944–45 (and on income above $200,000). After World War II, the top rate dropped back to 82 percent, but it jumped back to 92 percent during the Korean War. During the Vietnam War, the rate climbed from 70 percent in 1967 to 77 percent in 1969.[4] These examples reflect the observation of the American revolutionary Thomas Paine two centuries ago that "war . . . has but one thing certain, and that is to increase taxes."[5]

And yet, in the current war, the top rate of 39 percent in 2001, on incomes above approximately $300,000, is being modestly *reduced* by the Bush tax cuts. Other recent tax changes, discussed later in this chapter, also have the effect of making taxes less progressive than they were. So both in terms of cutting taxes and in terms of making them less progressive, the

Box 3 Who pays income taxes?

Income per return	Number of returns	Total income	Total tax paid
Under $50,000	70%	30%	15%
$50,000–100,000	20%	30%	25%
Over $100,000	10%	40%	60%
	100%	100%	100%

tax laws during this War on Terror run quite contrary to the historical pattern during wartime, which is to raise taxes, especially on the rich.

Paying Your Share

Each year in early April, millions of Americans gather their wits and checkbooks to pay their federal taxes—each hoping to minimize his or her own payment while still hoping to enjoy the benefits of everyone else's tax payments. Consider a hypothetical situation where some item on your tax return fell into a gray zone of tax law in which either of two interpretations were justifiable. The difference was that one interpretation made line 54—total income tax—$100 higher. Which would you choose? Law-abiding Americans have no obligation to pay more taxes than legally required. Anyway, what difference does $100 make in all those billions of tax dollars? And as the Republicans keep saying, "It's your money," not Washington's.

But suppose this $100 of taxes was paired with a particular expenditure, so that you were no longer invisible in a vast pool of people and funds but deciding the fate of your $100 bill in relation to a specific person or place. And suppose the recipients of your $100 were the parents of nineteen-year-old Diego Rincon in Conyers, Georgia, outside Atlanta. Rincon moved to the United States from Colombia at age five; excelled at drama, dance, and gymnastics in high school; joined the U.S. Army after 9/11; and was killed by a suicide bomber at a checkpoint in Iraq. He received U.S. citizenship posthumously.[6] Now put yourself in his parents' living room and tell them that you are keeping the $100 for yourself that the government promised them to help pay for their son's funeral. Here you wouldn't be able to shirk invisibly, blending into the crowd. But unfortunately, our tax dollars are not traceable as they disappear into the mass of government funds, so our own payment doesn't seem very important to the tasks that the government must accomplish, including the war.

Because of this problem, taxes would not work if they were voluntary. Instead, we have a government with the power to compel us to pay taxes. This is for our own good, though for some reason the public appreciates it less than you might think. By creating a central authority in the United States—the federal government—we are able as a society to accomplish tasks we could not accomplish as states, cities, or households. Among these tasks is defense against foreign threats. In the preamble to the U.S. Constitution, "We the people" set up the federal government for several purposes. "Provide for the common defense" is on the list, somewhere between establishing justice and promoting the general welfare.

William Lear of Muskegan, Michigan, did not want to pay federal income taxes, so he didn't. According to the IRS, Lear did not file a tax return for 1995 or 1996, when he earned gross receipts averaging over $90,000 per year from commissions on selling satellite dishes to homeowners. Lear claimed that Congress did not have legal authority to make him file a tax return, a position shared by other tax rebels. The judge and jury disagreed. In March 2003, Lear began a one-year sentence at the federal prison camp in Duluth, Minnesota. The IRS wants you to know that William Lear went to prison—it highlights his and similar cases on its Web site—just in case you were wondering whether to skip paying *your* taxes. The federal prison camp in Duluth thus serves as one solution to the problem of tax collection. With the mighty hand of the federal government reaching out to punish offenders, it is less feasible for individuals to cheat on social responsibilities.

While you are waiting in line at the post office to mail your tax return next April 14½, pick up a pamphlet at the counter on the way in. It says, "Men 18–25 Years, You Can Handle This." It tells them to register for the draft or be subject to penalties up to and including federal prison. In America's last sustained, multiyear war—Vietnam—as in every major American war, thousands of American men were compelled to join the armed forces and go fight. The draft has been necessary in most wars throughout history and around the world, because fighting in a war—like paying taxes—is not generally in the individual's self-interest but is often in the society's interest. The draft solves the problem of who will risk death protecting our society against foreign threats. But now we have solved that problem in a better way. We spend a lot to hire good soldiers, pay them decently (compared with a draftee), and train and equip them better than any army in history. In this way we have shifted some of the economic burden of war—of paying for security from foreign threats—away from the hapless draftees and onto a broader base of income tax payers. Today draft registration is largely symbolic. Draftees would just get in the way of the professional fighting forces as they do their jobs.

In our postdraft society, income taxes remain one of the few universal means by which ordinary American households contribute to the war effort. Tax historian W. Elliot Brownlee observes that taxes were raised in past wars, especially the Civil War and World War I, to "respond to some sense of shared sacrifice," but that "in this time of high-tech warfare and a volunteer Army, there is no longer the concern with equalizing sacrifice."[7] In truth, the issue of shared *economic* sacrifice is as salient today as ever. Especially now, when most middle-class and rich Americans do not fight, they should pay.

Here, then, is my modest proposal. Let's be happy about paying income tax. Let's imagine our money going straight to Diego Rincon's family. Let's raise taxes to pay for the war effort, as America has always done, and share the sacrifice fairly. And let's especially help rich Americans to participate more fully in their patriotic duty to help pay for our professional military and the new war-related expenses, as they have done in past wars.

Corporate Taxes

Although income taxes are far and away the federal government's most important source of funding, they are not the only source. Corporations also pay income taxes on their profits. These corporate income taxes used to be more important than they are now. In the 1950s they provided about 30 percent of the federal government's revenues, but since the 1980s that share is around 10 percent—much less than individual income taxes (which make up nearly 80 percent of the government's revenue). Congress lowered corporate tax rates in response to arguments that taxing both corporations and individuals amounts to double taxation of the same income and that high corporate taxes are bad for business.

Wartime has brought new public attention to corporations' tax obligations. For example, one method for legally avoiding taxes is to create "offshore" dummy companies in countries like Bermuda or the Cayman Islands, where there is no corporate income tax, and then manipulate financial transactions so that profits are reported in these tax-free venues. The corporate headquarters may be nothing more than a post office box. In recent years, a growing number of U.S. companies have used this "Bermuda loophole," costing the government $4 billion a year in lost revenue. For example, at the end of 2001 the industrial manufacturer Ingersoll-Rand moved its legal headquarters to Bermuda while its main office remained, as always, in Woodcliff Lake, New Jersey. By so doing, Ingersoll-Rand avoided paying more than $50 million per year in federal taxes.

After 9/11, as the country shifted to a wartime mentality, critics called the Bermuda-loophole companies unpatriotic. They pointed out that some of the companies avoiding payment of federal taxes were receiving federal contracts. For example, the IRS Web site mentioned earlier in this chapter is run by the giant consulting firm Accenture, headquartered in Bermuda. In 2002, Accenture also received hundreds of millions of dollars in federal contracts from the new Transportation Security Administration. In light of these criticisms, some members of Congress moved to eliminate the Bermuda loophole. The Senate passed such a law, but Republican leaders in the House killed it, saying they would not do anything to increase taxes. Similarly, in 2003 the manufacturing conglomerate Tyco voted down a shareholder resolution to move headquarters back to the United States from Bermuda, as did Ingersoll-Rand. However, the Connecticut toolmaker Stanley Works

gave up its plan to adopt the Bermuda loophole after encoun-
tering fierce public criticism.[8]

In mid-2003 an editorial in the local newspaper in Pittsfield,
Massachusetts, summed up corporate tax avoidance in wartime
as follows: "There are many ways for Americans to demon-
strate their patriotism, such as waving the flag and eating freedom fries. Perhaps the best way of showing patriotism is by
paying taxes, because it is our tax dollars that . . . pay the
salaries of our servicemen and women. . . . When the Senate
passed a modest bill to prevent the Homeland Security Department from doing business with companies that relocate overseas, that provision was removed by the Republican-dominated
House. Some of those who opposed the provision . . . are noted
practitioners of flag-waving and freedom fry–consuming, but
when it comes to helping the large corporations that have
bought the GOP, self-interest comes before patriotism."[9]

The Bush administration once did ask corporations for a
little help with increasing tax revenues. It was just before
9/11, and the White House said that large corporations would
not mind sending in $5 billion in federal taxes two weeks
early (which would help the government meet a certain budget goal). Press Secretary Ari Fleischer explained that for corporations, "It's just a short number of days, really." The response from Corporate America was straightforward. As the
director of tax policy for the accounting company Deloitte and
Touche put it, "There is zero chance any member of the For-
tune 100 would ever pay corporate taxes ahead of time. Corporations do not have the slightest interest in paying corporate taxes early. They're not going to volunteer money to the
government." Any corporate financial executive who sent millions of dollars to the government two weeks early would be
fired, he added.[10]

Clearly, this war will need financial support from all sources. The rigid Republican stand against all "tax increases," by preventing Congress from closing loopholes or even raising corporate tax rates modestly, leaves the funding of the war short, with consequences that will be discussed in Chapters 8–11.

Excise Taxes

As the saying goes, "a billion here, a billion there—pretty soon you're talking real money."[11] The billions here and there that the federal government collects as excise taxes are a third, though much smaller, source of revenue after personal income taxes and corporate income taxes. (In addition, the government takes in some money from other sources, such as tariffs on certain imported goods.) Excise taxes apply to dozens of specific categories of purchases, ranging from gasoline and airplane tickets to phone calls and luxury goods. Their beauty, politically, is that they are almost invisible to the public.

About half the excise tax comes from gasoline and diesel fuel. The rest is split more or less four ways between alcohol, tobacco, air travel, and telephone services. The excise taxes go into the big pool of government revenue along with income taxes, and war costs are paid out of that pool. But most of the excise taxes are keyed to specific areas of expenditure, mostly not war related. The big tax, on fuel, is tied to the maintenance of the highway system and therefore best excluded in thinking about where war funds come from. Similarly, though less directly, taxes on alcohol and tobacco are connected with federal health programs such as medical research. The air transportation tax seems somewhat related to the War on Terror, since the government is spending a lot more on air transportation security since 9/11. For every flight segment, the federal government gets 7.5 percent of the fare plus $3. But that rate is only slightly higher than before 9/11 and traditionally helps pay for the whole federal aviation system, not just security upgrades.[12]

Next time you drop fifty cents in a pay phone—if you can still find one—take note that a penny and a half goes to the federal government as an excise tax historically tied to war. Each month, 3 percent is added to your phone bill, as well as to phone cards and pay calls. The phone company collects it for the government and passes it along to the IRS. Didn't know you were paying a federal tax on phone services? As I said: almost invisible, politically beautiful. The monthly tab per household is only $5, 1 percent of what the war system runs on, but it adds up to $6 billion a year for the government.

The phone tax as a war tax has a history dating back a century. It was created by the War Revenue Act of 1898 to help pay for the Spanish-American War and lasted for three years. The original tax, one cent per phone call, was conceived as a luxury excise tax, since telephones were then a luxury for the rich. During World War I, the phone tax was reinstated. It was dropped in 1924 and reinstated six years later. The rates tripled in 1942, doubled again in 1943, and doubled again by 1945. The phone tax was collected all during the Cold War and stood at 10 percent during the Vietnam War, after which it was lowered to the present 3 percent rate.[13] The phone tax is a "regressive" tax, taking a larger share of income from the poor than from the rich, since the poor pay a higher percentage of their total income for phone service.

Pacifists who oppose paying taxes to support military purposes have long used the phone tax as a symbolic target of their resistance. It turns out the phone company generally can't shut off your phone service for nonpayment—it is between you and the IRS. But since the amounts are so small, it would be too expensive for the IRS to come after you to collect. Some war tax resisters withhold the federal tax on their phone bill and donate it to charitable groups instead. Although this symbolic protest has only the tiniest effect on the funding of war, it may have been enough of an annoyance that in 1990 the phone tax was made permanent and declared, arbitrarily, to be in support of child-care spending. The same money still goes the same places, but the phone tax is no longer officially called a war tax.

The 1990s saw an excise tax imposed on "luxury cars." It applied to the amount of a new car's price above $40,000. The tax on that amount started at 10 percent in 1990 but was phased down to 3 percent by 2002. Thus, for example, a personal car bought for $50,000—business vehicles were exempt—would have been taxed at 3 percent of $10,000, or an additional $300, collected by the car dealer on behalf of Uncle Sam. The tax produced nearly $3 billion during its twelve-year lifetime, but it expired in 2003.[14] The income lost to the federal government is small potatoes on the national scale, but somewhere the federal government will need to find—meaning borrow, in the short term—several hundred million dollars each year that buyers of expensive cars used to pay. Again, the effect of these tax changes is to shift the relative tax burden away from the rich and onto the poor or future generations.

Estate and gift taxes affect the rich almost exclusively. Gift tax revenues—on transfers of tens of thousands of dollars or more—were cut from $4 billion in 2001 to under $2 billion in 2002, just as the nation went to a war footing. Meanwhile, the Republicans pushed to eliminate the estate tax on inheritances, which they call the "death tax," altogether. Estate taxes provided more than $20 billion a year of revenue in recent years. The first tax on inheritance helped fund the Civil War. It "passed Congress with little debate because of the widespread demand in the North for sacrifice, especially from the wealthy," writes journalist Steven Weisman.[15] As an average across all U.S. households, the estate and gift taxes come to more than $15 a month; but for the great majority of households these taxes total zero, and for the few they come to a lot more than $15 a month. If the rich are no longer taxed, the poor and middle class will be paying more of this $15 a month themselves, one way or another. Like the phone tax, estate and gift taxes go into the general fund of the government, supporting both military and nonmilitary expenses.

Thus, regressive excise taxes—on phones and gasoline—remain unchanged, while progressive ones such as those on luxury cars and very large gifts have been drastically reduced or eliminated. Again, such a regressive trend runs counter to the government's actions in past wars, when it has tapped the resources of the rich most heavily to pay for war. Just as Willie Sutton said he robbed banks because "that's where the money is," so does the federal government turn to rich Americans in time of war to pay the lion's share. But not this time.

Follow the Money

Let's follow the money as it flows from your household into the federal government—and additional money is borrowed—to be spent for both war and domestic purposes. I express all the amounts on a monthly per-household basis, even though some taxes are only indirectly connected to households, as when members of the household perhaps work for companies that pay corporate taxes.

Box 4 shows where the government gets its money—rounded off, per household, per month—and how it spends it.

Box 4 The money trail.
Income taxes are the most important source of war funds.

UNITED STATES GOVERNMENT
WASHINGTON, D.C.

The Smith Household
12345 Main St.
Anytown, USA

Dear Smith Household:

It's your money! Here's where the government gets your share of its budget:

Individual income tax	**$700/month**
Corporation tax	100
Excise taxes	50
Other*	50
Subtotal	$900/month
Borrowed from Social Security surplus	150
Borrowed on the open market	350
Total available for general expenditures**	**$1,400/month**

And here's where that money goes:

War-related spending (see Box 2 on p. 16)	**$500/month**
Needs-based programs such as Medicaid	300
Nonmilitary federal agencies and programs	300
Most of interest on debt and misc.***	300
Total	**$1,400/month**

* In addition, excluded here, the government collects more than $150 per household monthly in fees that offset expenses within the agencies that collect them (e.g., national parks).
** Excludes Social Security and Medicare trust funds. The government collects almost $600 a month in payroll taxes, of which about $150 is a surplus.
*** Excludes $40/month of the debt interest already included under war-related spending.

Although this description is terribly oversimplified, it gives the big picture.[16]

To summarize, the most important source of money for the government's war-related spending is income taxes. Your own household's income taxes ultimately fund wartime spending. Yet, the same middle- and upper-class Americans who pay the most income tax, and therefore usually are the main funders of war-related spending, are receiving sizable tax cuts just as security costs escalate—a shift away from progressive income taxes as the main source of war funding through history. This trend away from a progressive tax for war is amplified by cuts in other taxes on the rich, such as estate and excise taxes. The current policy of reducing taxes in wartime while making them more regressive takes more of the costs of the War on Terror from the pocketbooks of poor and middle-class Americans and is a historically unique experiment. It is an experiment doomed to failure.

Chapter Three

BUDGET CUTS

The second main way we are funding war, in addition to tax revenues, is debt. But before turning to that topic, which leads on to inflation and wider effects on society, let's consider a third source—cutting other programs in the federal, state, and local budgets. The amounts are not as large, but these cuts directly affect our quality of life.

Government budget cuts deserve our attention here for two reasons. First, this war, unlike previous ones, has put large new war-related burdens on domestic agencies funded by state and local governments, such as police and fire departments. Second, as the resources and attention of government at all levels shift toward war needs, they inevitably shift away from domestic needs. Cuts to government services caused by the recession are made worse by the new wartime demands on governmental budgets. Resources shifted away from social programs are taken at the expense of the vulnerable segments of society such as children, the elderly, and the poor.

The War on Terror has placed new, unique demands on local and state governments, whose budgets already were under strain. These demands include many new unfunded federal mandates. Police, firefighters, and hospitals need more funding—for new training, equipment, and personnel—to cope with the new threats to American cities. But local governments are short of funds for these purposes, and state and federal governments have not supplied the money in amounts that would compensate for local shortfalls. So local and state governments, which already faced a severe budget crisis, must cut services and raise taxes and fees even more to meet these new wartime demands.

Certainly, war is not the main cause of the budget cuts now devastating programs and services at the federal, state, and local levels. Most of the cuts are at the state and local levels, generally not competing directly with the major costs of war, which are in the federal budget. But the war does make the situation worse.

Federal Programs

Let's start with the federal budget, where war spending competes directly with other line items. President Bush's 2005 budget proposal is explicit about this competition: "Since September 11, 2001, more than three-quarters of the increase in discretionary spending has been directly related to our response to the attacks, enhanced homeland security, and the War on Terror. The President's 2005 Budget continues this spending trend: significant increases in funding our security programs combined with a dramatic reduction in the growth of discretionary spending unrelated to security."[1]

Although much smaller than the state and local cuts—because most programs and services in our lives are funded by states and cities—cuts to federal programs also affect local communities. Most poignant of these budget shortfalls were those affecting citizen participation in national service in 2003.

AmeriCorps

AmeriCorps is a federal program that places college-age volunteers in community service for up to a year, in exchange for about $5,000 in college tuition, a modest stipend, child care, and health insurance. Boston college student Shavon Lynch thought that tutoring a five-year-old from a troubled family for ten hours a week through an AmeriCorps-funded work-study program called Jumpstart was "the best thing I've ever done." Her partner child, James, had been angry—his mother in jail until he was three, then living with him, then gone again. He used words sparingly but fists abundantly, played with few children, and showed little interest in reading or writing. Lynch read to him, drew pictures with him, sang with him, let him know someone cared about him. "James is a different child now, he's not so angry at the world anymore," Lynch says, and he has built the skills to start kindergarten.[2]

With today's young people fired up to serve the country after 9/11—and too few jobs for them upon college graduation anyway—this program should be expanding rapidly. Certainly, you would expect so from listening to President Bush's 2002 State of the Union address. He invoked the spirit of service felt by many Americans over the previous four months and promised to "expand and improve the good efforts of Ameri-

Corps." Later he explained that this meant going from fifty thousand to seventy-five thousand volunteers.

The day after the address, a White House press briefing featured John Bridgeland, the director of AmeriCorps's parent organization, USA Freedom Corps. He said there would be twenty-five thousand new AmeriCorps participants receiving stipends and small college grants, funded by a total program budget of $230 million. A reporter asked, "How much of any of this happening depends on Congress coming up with some money?" Bridgeland talked about something else. Later the reporter asked again, "So the President can't do anything of this unilaterally, he needs Congress to come up with the money? Which is, I guess, the question I was asking before." Bridgeland answered, "We're going to work . . . to get this legislation to Congress so we both authorize and then fund these programs."[3]

But they didn't, although the president's party controlled both houses of Congress. In fall 2003, Shavon Lynch's Jumpstart position was terminated. Congress severely cut the AmeriCorps budget in 2003, and the number of volunteers dropped sharply. In Rochester, New York, the local AmeriCorps office, whose one hundred members provided 150,000 hours of service to community organizations each year, prepared to shut down altogether in 2004 unless new funds materialized.[4] Supporters appealed to Bush and Congress to pass a supplemental appropriation of $185 million, fifteen cents per household monthly, to restore AmeriCorps to the status quo—never mind expanding it, as President Bush had promised. But Congress would not. As a result, tens of thousands of young, idealistic Americans who had signed up and been accepted for AmeriCorps programs such as Jumpstart were sent away without work or pay in fall 2003 and "told they can't serve their country," as columnist Jonathan Alter put it (see Box 5). Lynch told

Box 5 Impact of budget cuts on AmeriCorps.

Change in number of AmeriCorps volunteers promised by President Bush, 2002:
+25,000

Change in number of AmeriCorps volunteers funded by Congress, 2003:
–20,000

Note: Congress funded the president's promise in 2004, so the new volunteers will be on the job during election year. Perhaps those turned away in 2003 will reapply.

a press conference, "If I could say anything to President Bush—it would be this: We have answered your call to service—300,000 of us [since 1992] have stepped forward to serve our communities and our nation. Please don't deny us that opportunity."[5]

As Congress was letting the last chance for AmeriCorps slip by in 2003, Dave Eggers, who founded a volunteer tutoring program in San Francisco, wrote that "it was the president's words" in the State of the Union speech "that encouraged young people to send in AmeriCorps applications," because they wanted to do "something selfless for a country that needed healing." AmeriCorps, he wrote, "has become, for an entire generation, the model for service." Now, "a generation that was beginning to engage with government, with citizenship and service, will be abandoned. . . . In fact, the best and most idealistic members of this generation are the ones who will feel most betrayed."[6] At the end of 2003, Congress finally agreed to provide the large funding boost for AmeriCorps, so more volunteers can go to work during 2004—election year.

But the AmeriCorps expansion, like so much else in the first two years of the War on Terror, faces an uncertain future after a rough start.

Citizen Corps

Of the various volunteer service programs promoted but left underfunded, the most directly relevant to war needs is the new Citizen Corps.

Two months after 9/11, in an address to the nation from Atlanta, President Bush took up the question that critics found unanswered in his earlier policies: Can't ordinary citizens do more to help the war than just go shopping? "Many ask, what can I do to help in our fight," Bush noted. "The answer is simple. All of us can become a September the 11th volunteer by making a commitment to service in our own communities." He praised efforts like "children across America [who] have organized lemonade and cookie sales for children in Afghanistan."[7] (Given the importance of funding for Afghanistan, children might seem an odd source, but President Bush had asked them the previous month to contribute.)

Bush listed other ways to participate: tutoring a child, comforting the afflicted, housing the homeless, participating in Neighborhood Watch, volunteering in a hospital or rescue unit, supporting troops through the United Service Organizations (USO). "Our citizens have new responsibilities," Bush said. "Obviously, we must inspect our mail, and stay informed on public health matters" (this was right after the mailed anthrax incidents).[8] A month earlier, a reporter asked Bush, "What are Americans supposed to look for and report to the police or to the FBI?" He answered, "Well, Ann, you know, if you find a person that you've never seen before getting in a crop duster that doesn't belong to you—report it."[9] The wording may be tangled, but we get the idea. Still, all these efforts seemed scattered and impromptu, and the administration in late 2001 pulled them together under a new name, Citizen Corps, announced in the same State of the Union address in which the president promised the expansion of AmeriCorps. By April 2002, Bush could give a much more specific answer to what Americans should do to help the war: "And so for those of you out there who are interested in participating, I want you to call up this number, 1-877-USA-CORPS, or to dial up on the Internet, www.citizencorps.gov. This is a way where you can help America."[10]

One year later, although many cities and states had established Citizen Corps councils, Manhattan borough president C. Virginia Fields found it "extremely discouraging" that New York City's could not get off the ground. Her constituents, living in the city most at risk, were eager to get involved in homeland security, she said, but the money to make it happen wasn't there. After the speeches were over, the Bush administration had given just $25 million nationwide—two cents per household monthly—for Citizen Corps, of which only $4 million was for grants to the councils. New York State's share was supposed to be about $1 million, but by April 2003 the governor's office had not even developed the guidelines for councils to apply for it, and two different New York City councils were competing for the scant funds. Here's how the governor's spokeswoman put it: "We haven't been able to move forward as quickly as we hoped in this process because of a difference in opinion between the mayor's office and the Manhattan borough president's office over the division of resources." Fields herself put it more succinctly: "We have ignored all this interest at the local level. It's absolutely backwards. The whole thing is wrongheaded."[11] Had the federal government adequately funded Bush's promises of a year and a half earlier, New York residents might have somewhere to put their volunteer energies, and we might have a new weapon in the War on Terror instead of a political squabble.

Veterans

Next, consider federal funding for veterans. Congress cut $28 billion over ten years from the budget for veterans' benefits. The veterans already paid with their service in past wars, and now Congress is cutting back on the government's end of the deal. Veterans must now pay a new $250 enrollment fee to start using the Veterans Affairs (VA) hospital system, for example.

In Leeds, Massachusetts, a private nonprofit organization runs a shelter for homeless veterans on the grounds of the VA hospital. The program lost $500,000 in federal funding and nearly had to close half of its 120 beds—which were being used to full capacity—and cut its programs to help veterans cope with mental illness, substance abuse, and finding jobs. The shelter scraped along in 2003 with a $36,000 grant from a foundation, the Disabled American Veterans Charitable Service Trust.[12] As with the new $250 enrollment fee, costs like the shelter's budget that used to be paid by all taxpayers have shifted to private groups and individuals.

Other Programs

Other federal programs face cutbacks as well. President Bush was trying, in 2003, to shift responsibility for the highly acclaimed federally funded preschool program, Head Start, to the states—where it would compete with other programs in the besieged state budgets. "We think it would absolutely destroy Head Start," said Sarah Greene, leader of the nonprofit National Head Start Association.[13] The federal government was also cutting back the Low Income Home Energy Assistance Program (LIHEAP), which provided help with heating oil for people too poor to heat their homes during harsh winters. Most of those people vote Democratic anyway, if they vote at all, so there's little harm to Republicans in cutting their energy assistance. Cuts also were planned for other programs that benefit more Democrats than Republicans—food stamps, school lunch and nutrition programs, school nurses, and others.

Health Care

The health care sector has been hit hard, from the federal to the local level. Yet health resources would be critically important in responding to either a conventional attack or a biological, chemical, or nuclear one. For instance, if terrorists attacked downtown Chicago, Jackson Park Hospital on the South Side, about six miles away, would be on the front line of the war. It is a large, 326-bed facility that normally serves a population of a million people. But Cook County Board of Commissioners member Roberto Maldonado, a psychologist, did not like what he saw on two visits to patients at Jackson Park Hospital in 2003—mice. He told the board, "It was deplorable. These mice were so comfortable, they wouldn't move if you chased them." The Board of Commissioners president responded that Jackson Park was "as clean as most hospitals. There were mice and roaches at County [Hospital]." A staff person from a hospital accreditation group told the *Chicago Tribune* that a mouse infestation is a serious problem at any hospital because rodents spread disease: "Not having mice is as fundamental as a hospital having running water." In explaining why the Health Department had not inspected the hospital, despite a complaint about the mice three months earlier, the deputy director of the department said, "It's a long process and we deal with lots of complaints."[14]

Budget cuts trimmed the resources of the Chicago Department of Public Health in 2000–2003. At the same time, threats of biological weapons attacks created big new demands on the department's existing resources. Similarly, Jackson Park Hospital had fewer resources to deal with the mice, much less deal with casualties of a terrorist attack, because of budget cuts in Medicaid and other health programs by the city of Chicago, the state of Illinois, and the federal government.

Dr. Irwin Redlener, director of the disaster preparedness center in Columbia University's school of public health, said in 2003, "Now, nearly two years after 9/11, the hospitals and public health systems are absolutely unprepared for another major act of terrorism. There's been very little improvement from two years ago."[15]

Medicaid

Medicaid uses state funds and matching federal funds to cover the health care costs of low-income people. (A related program through the states provides children's health insurance.) Medicaid expenses have grown rapidly—by around 15 percent in 2001 and 7 percent in 2002—as have most health-sector costs.[16] The recession lowered incomes, making more people eligible for Medicaid, and Medicaid cushioned the impact of the recession in 2001 by providing health coverage for some of the millions of Americans who lost private health insurance. But many states were short of funds for the program, and the Republican leadership in the House of Representatives proposed cuts in the federal funds.

Medicaid cuts translated into loss of health care coverage by recipients. In Massachusetts and Florida, Medicaid stopped paying for eyeglasses, hearing aids, and artificial limbs. Children's Hospital of Pittsburgh announced that it expected to lose nearly $7 million from Medicaid budget cuts approved by the Pennsylvania legislature in 2003 as part of a package of $250 million in health care cuts. In September 2003, hundreds of thousands of Texas children lost their Children's Health Insurance.[17]

Ronnie Gonzalez of Jersey City, New Jersey, lost his health benefits after being laid off from the electronics retailer The Wiz in 2002. The state insurance plan had just been discontinued, and the next year his unemployment compensation ran out. He needed $800 a month in medicine for hepatitis C. When he needed $300 for antibiotics, he told the local newspaper, "I had to take that from money I saved for the rent. And bills are still coming in." Gonzalez's three children, ages one to eight, still had health coverage through a state plan, but that plan was threatened by state budget cuts in the coming years.[18]

The health care coverage crisis was not caused by war. But without the war, the federal government could be covering more of the health care services being lost. It could be funneling money to hospitals and city health departments, *increasing* Medicaid funding since there are more people in need and health costs are rising per person. The federal government could be using the nation's resources and energies, now diverted to wartime tasks such as homeland security, to strengthen the social safety net.

State Budget Crises

As serious as the situation is for Medicaid, it is just one piece of a larger picture of money troubles across the fifty state governments—"a rising tide of red ink, as far as the eye can see," to quote an Atlanta analyst's report to a Federal Reserve committee in 2003. The National Conference of State Legislatures estimated the total budget gap in fiscal year 2004 for all the states, even after the federal bailout of 2003, at about $50 billion. The executive director of the National Governors' Association called it "the worst budget crisis states have faced since World War II. They can't run deficits, so they must cut services. They avoid cuts to public safety, especially because of terrorist threats, and so the cuts fall mostly on services to poor people, and the rest on services to everyone—dispensable things like libraries, environmental protection, health services, and the like."[19]

Journalist Nicholas Kristof wrote of returning to his hometown, Yamhill, Oregon, in 2003. He found "a real, measurable drop in the quality of life here." The schools had laid off teachers, increased class sizes, and slashed foreign-language instruction. Other nearby districts had to close schools early to save money, and in one town the police department was eliminated. The county cut out funding for prenatal care, mental health, and the jail's successful drug abuse program. When Missouri apprehended a criminal wanted in Oregon for stealing hundreds of thousands of dollars, they had to free him because Oregon decided it could not afford to bring him back for trial.[20]

Money to maintain highways also fell victim to the budget cuts. Keeping up roads, bridges, and other infrastructure can be postponed a few years, but it is catching up with us. During a period of high unemployment, it would be useful for the government to put money into highways and other infrastructure projects, to create jobs. But that would mean less money for tax cuts and for the war.

Many state colleges and universities hiked tuition rates steeply, in addition to laying off workers, increasing class sizes, and instituting a host of cost-saving, service-reducing measures. If you can't afford tuition at a state school, you may miss out on a college education. These are all costs resulting from the state budget cuts that citizens must pay in return for not paying even more state taxes.

The list goes on and on. Nebraska raised state college tuition 20 percent in two years, and took away health care coverage from twenty-five thousand poor mothers. In Missouri, the governor ordered every third light bulb unscrewed to save on electric bills. Indiana closed campgrounds. In Oklahoma, teachers took over janitorial duties and bus driving. Pleasant Ridge, Michigan, planned to sell advertising space on the side of police patrol cars.[21]

The war didn't cause these state budget crises. But it makes them much worse by diverting the nation's attention and resources.

Homeland security costs are the most direct way that this war hurts state and local budgets. In New York City, the antiterrorist program Operation Atlas costs an estimated $700 million a year. The mayor asked Congress to pay—it would come to fifty-five cents a month per household nationally—but Congress offered only $200 million. The rest, half a billion dollars, comes out of the New York City budget, one way or another. Constitutional law professor Jason Mazzone, from Brooklyn, argues that the federal government should pay the whole bill. The Constitution, he notes, says that "the United States . . . shall protect each of [the states] against Invasion"—a term that the founders understood to mean sneak attacks by secret agents as well as open assault by gunships and invading armies. When the states ceded power to the federal government in matters of war, treaties, and foreigners, they received in return the promise of federal protection, not just for the country as a whole but for "each" of the states. "A particular state must not be left vulnerable just because taxpayers in other states prefer not to contribute additional money needed for its protection. . . . The Constitution does not allow the federal government simply to leave it up to the states to protect themselves from terrorist attacks." Mazzone concludes that "if New York City needs Operation Atlas, the federal government must pay for the program." Until Congress agrees, however, New York has to keep cutting its budget to pay for homeland security expenses including those mandated by the federal government.[22]

States have used various gimmicks to deal with budget shortfalls. They have tapped—and depleted—"rainy-day funds" built up in the 1990s and money from the settlement of a huge lawsuit against tobacco companies. States have sold off buildings and leased them back. They have shifted paydays to borrow a month from the next fiscal year—a trick you can use only once. New Jersey governor James McGreevey (a Democrat) used that trick in 2003 after cutting the budget by $3 billion, raising corporate taxes by $1 billion, and draining the state tobacco settlement money and "every state fund with a positive balance," to quote the *Washington Post*. To get the last needed reduction of $300 million, he ordered a June payment to New Jersey's school districts to be shifted to July 1, the new fiscal year. But sixty-six districts could not make contractually required payments to teachers in June without the state money. The shift leaves the 2004 budget short $300 million, requiring another shift to July 1 the next year just to stay even. "We will be one payment behind forevermore," one state senator said. Meanwhile, in Florida, the legislature took more than

$1 billion from trust funds and saving accounts to close the gap in 2003, another one-time fix.[23]

In the midst of this depressing scene, the federal government did come through in mid-2003 with funds to help the states. The bailout payment was the most that Democrats, and a few moderate Republicans, could extract from the Republican leadership as the price of allowing the much larger 2003 tax cuts to pass. The bailout consisted of $10 billion over fifteen months, intended to help Medicaid, and another $10 billion over two years for general purposes—totaling $10 a month per average American household. It was too little and too late, but the funds could help preserve some services desperately needed by poor people and children. However, no sooner had the federal funds been announced than armies of lobbyists descended on state capitals to divide the new pie, with the intended recipients—poor people and children—distinctly underrepresented in the process. In Massachusetts, the executive director of the state Municipal Association argued for giving the funds to cities and towns to provide citizens with services such as public safety and education. But health care advocates wanted to spend it on restoring Medicaid cuts. The Democratic legislative leaders in Massachusetts, like the Republican governor of Florida, proposed to set aside the bailout money for the next year's budget, taking a hit in 2003 to have something left for 2004, which happens to be an election year.[24]

Military pressures on the federal budget restrained effective aid to the states as they weathered their budget crises. Consider that in 2003 Congress reluctantly passed $20 billion for two years of aid to states, and overwhelmingly passed $80 billion for half a year's supplemental costs of the Iraq campaign and the War on Terror. Suppose these two were reversed. I am not saying they should have been—it is wartime—but suppose they could have been. The aid to states could then have balanced all the state budgets and forestalled most of the budget cuts in health, education, and other areas. Wartime thus worsens the devastating cuts in state programs and services.

Local Governments

As go the states, so go the cities and towns. Local services are eroding across the land. As new homeland security demands compete with other local budget items, and as the federal and state governments grow stingier, local communities feel the pain in their understaffed schools and police and fire departments, their increasing local and state tax bills, and their unrepaired potholes and crumbling bridges.

Cities and towns face new mandates and needs related to homeland security that are unfunded by federal and state governments. These extend far beyond the first responders—police, fire, and medical personnel. Oklahoma City, which has firsthand experience with terrorism, installed 181 new sirens to alert citizens in an emergency. Decades ago, all our cities had sirens in case of nuclear attack—770 in New York, 400 in Washington, D.C., and 225 in Los Angeles. The federal government paid for this system. But now, as several cities build or resurrect systems of sirens on lampposts, they are on their own. Oklahoma City residents will pay the $5 million cost of their new sirens, and other new expenses, through a voter-approved sales tax increase.[25]

The U.S. Conference of Mayors, Democrats and Republicans together, complained in September 2003 that almost all the federal aid for counterterrorism (several billion dollars in all) had been grabbed by state governments, with little left for cities. James A. Garner—president of the conference, mayor of Hempstead, New York, and a Republican—told a news conference, "9-1-1 does not ring at the statehouse; it rings at city hall." In April 2003, and again in December 2003, when the terror alert level rose, the Conference of Mayors estimated that cities faced $70 million a week in added costs as a result.[26]

Houston's 2004 budget was $59 million short in revenue to cover expenses. Like other cities, Houston cut back on child health services, clinics, libraries, and community centers. The *Houston Chronicle* noted that "government services for the poor are most affected by budget cuts because they are among the most expensive programs and because their recipients are less likely to retaliate in the voting booth."[27]

In many transit districts nationally, fares for public transportation increased in 2003. In Springfield, Massachusetts, they went from seventy-five cents to a dollar to help close a $3 million deficit in the local transit agency's budget. A frustrated senior citizen advocate, Frank Wells, complained, "They're putting the whole burden of the state's financial woes on those who can least afford to pay." The Metro public transportation system in Washington, D.C., projected a $50 million deficit for 2003, and New York City's transportation authority projected deficits in the hundreds of millions of dollars. Transportation expert Elizabeth Deakin, a University of California, Berkeley, professor, explained: "You have a confluence of security costs and a bad economy that makes it tough for these agencies to keep their commitments." The Golden Gate Bridge authority, which added nearly a million dollars a year in new security personnel to cope with potential terrorist threats, faced a deficit of $60 million per year and projected bankruptcy early in 2004. It raised tolls from $3 to $5, cut bus routes, and installed collection boxes for pedestrians and bicyclists to make voluntary contributions.[28]

Education

As budget cuts trickle down to America's communities, the last stop is the school district, where local officials cut programs to try to balance budgets with less local, state, and federal funding. In Texas, cuts planned to public education topped $1 billion in 2003, money that local districts had no way to make up. Houston's school district cut $3 million from its famed magnet programs, which include Arabic language training—a desperate need in post-9/11 America. The executive director of the American Association of School Administrators said that the war effort and the tax cuts combined to harm public education, specifically the reforms championed by President Bush but then inadequately funded. (Although the federal budget for the Education Department increased about one-quarter in 2001–3, to $50 billion, Representative George Miller, D-Calif., a cowriter of the federal education reform legislation, accused President Bush of budgeting nearly $10 billion less than needed to carry out promised education reform.)[29]

In South Carolina, the teacher of the year in 2002, Traci Young Cooper, had her position in the district—working with teachers to meet standards—eliminated in 2003 when the state legislature reduced school funding sharply. Cooper said she understood that the legislature had "to make tough choices. But in the forefront of their minds should be the children, and at the state funding levels they're providing now, I don't think that's a reality." The budget crises of school districts, aggravated by wartime economics, reach down into the pockets of schoolteachers, who have long been expected to buy supplies for their classrooms out of their own money. Indeed, de facto pay cuts for teachers take many forms, from extra janitorial duties, to higher co-payments for health visits, to the two weeks that Oregon teachers worked without pay in 2003.[30]

This war also places demands on school districts that distract from educating the children. A 2003 report from the National Association of School Resource Officers, based on a survey of seven hundred school safety officials, found that three-quarters considered their schools—a likely "soft target" for terrorists—inadequately protected. The report found "no significant changes in emergency preparedness and training" since 9/11.[31]

When changes do occur, they take money and time from the schools' mission. Houston superintendent of schools Kaye Stripling sent a letter to parents in 2003 explaining the shelter-in-place procedures schools would use "in case of chemical or biological release." Every school has emergency plans, principals have reviewed procedures with staff, and school officials have met with law enforcement and other government agencies, she explained.[32] Parents no doubt were glad to hear it. But clearly, the school district's money and personnel time spent preparing for a possible attack on Houston did *not* go for educating children. The demands of war within agencies and jurisdictions such as the Houston school district—and there are thousands of them across the country—impede the delivery of services. This negative impact is in addition to actual budget cuts. Such impacts do not get counted in economic statistics.

In summary, wartime demands on the federal budget compete with domestic federal programs and, more important, restrain effective federal aid to cities and states. Budget cuts pass along to Americans, especially the poor, part of the cost of war not being paid by income taxes. In the big picture, however, budget cuts involve smaller sums of money than war spending, income taxes, or new federal deficits.

Chapter Four

DEBT

Dear Ms. Jane Q. Smith:

Congratulations! Because of your good credit rating, your household has qualified for a $500 loan to help pay this month's bills. Just sign and deposit the enclosed check made out in your name, and you're off to a good start on your month. Best of all, we will send you another $500 check each month to help make your life a little easier. We're here for you!

—Your National Debt Credit Card Company

P.S. Terms of credit card agreement apply to each $500 increase in your balance.

Should Jane Smith take the $500? If she takes it this month, should she then take it every month? Jane's family could certainly use the money. Expenses are up in recent years. Her household's share of war-related spending is up $150 a month since 9/11 (on top of $350 a month), just as Jane's monthly bill for home security would go up if she leased a fancy alarm system after being burglarized. Jane's family health bills are up too, in recent years. But her real wages (her wages adjusted for inflation) have been shrinking a bit since 2001. It is tempting to sign the $500 check, do it every month, and have magic money suddenly appear to pay the bills.

The $500 check to Jane's family (the average U.S. household) adds up to the federal budget deficit—that is, how much more the federal government spends than it takes in each month—which is Jane's share of the increase in the national debt each month. (It is a coincidence that the budget deficit in 2003 roughly equaled government war-related spending at $500 a month per household.) In 2003, this estimate of the deficit (including what we borrow from Social Security and Medicare surpluses) changed frequently, always upward, as new tax cuts and supplemental war spending bills were enacted. By the time you read this, Jane may be getting an even bigger monthly check. The White House budget in January 2004 projected a deficit in 2005 that would amount to nearly $600 per household monthly.

What I mean by the deficit is the *on-budget* deficit, before the government borrows from the Social Security and Medicare trust funds and calls the result a "unified budget." This on-budget deficit rose in 2003 to $500 per household monthly, coming to 5.7 percent of the Gross Domestic Product (GDP, measuring the whole U.S. economy). The deficit is about $180 lower per household monthly if you consider only the "unified budget" and ignore the growing pile of IOUs to the Social Security and Medicare trust funds.

Is There a Problem?

Each year that the government spends more than it takes in, it creates a budget deficit, and the national debt increases by that amount. Should we be alarmed about the deficits? You can look at it two ways, neither completely without truth. On one side, supporters of high deficits say that the on-budget deficits still amount to only 6 percent of GDP, a small slice of the total economy. We've had deficits nearly that high before without terrible damage; let's not get hysterical about them. Jane Q. Smith can make the payments on both her mortgage and the national debt—provided her income holds out.

The deficit has grown so rapidly in recent years for three reasons—recession, war, and tax cuts. Since Republicans see tax cuts as a growth stimulant, they believe that a growing economy could carry, and someday pay down, the debts now being incurred. During wartime and during recession, deficit spending is the best policy to keep the economy on track, they argue. This argument has some merit. Keynesian economic principles support the idea of using deficit spending to get through a difficult period such as war or recession. This must be a short-term strategy, however.[1]

On the other side, the debt is now growing quickly, and interest payments are eating up 20 percent of the federal budget, excluding Social Security and Medicare. Since 2001 the federal budget has flipped out of balance more dramatically than ever before in our history. In 2001 the nonpartisan Congressional Budget Office (CBO) projected that the unified budget *surplus* (including Social Security and Medicare surpluses) would exceed $350 billion in 2003, and amount to $5.6 trillion over ten years—enough to pay off the whole national debt and cover the baby boomers' retirement benefits. Just two years later, the actual fiscal-year 2003 surplus (unified budget) was instead a *deficit* of $375 billion, and the projected 2004 deficit was around $500 billion, with the CBO estimating that for the next ten years deficits would total $4 trillion. So the outlook for the coming decade reversed by nearly $10 trillion in just two years. To put it in terms of Jane's monthly bills, in 2001 she was actually paying down her National Debt Credit Card balance by $100 a month, but in early 2004 she was running up the balance $500 higher each month.

Writ large across 105 million households like Jane's, "the budget outlook has undergone the swiftest and largest reversal in our history," in the words of the Concord Coalition, a non-partisan organization devoted to balanced federal budgets. The coalition warns that despite this "dramatic deterioration," most politicians "are pushing the same free-lunch agendas"—especially "supply-side conservatives eager to tax less and big-government liberals eager to spend more." The Concord Coalition does have a track record: In June 2000, President Bill Clinton announced a nearly $2 trillion projected federal budget surplus over the coming ten years. As Republicans pushed to give it away as tax cuts, and Democrats to spend it on programs, the coalition warned, "We don't know whether this projected surplus will ever materialize." They called that one.[2]

Economic history writer John Steele Gordon warned in 1997 that the run-up of debt over fifteen years—spending "as much of tomorrow's money as . . . fighting a major war," despite the relative peace and prosperity of the period—would leave us at a disadvantage "if, tomorrow, the country actually has to fight one." (Now we do.) And this debt accumulated "for no better reason, when it comes right down to it, than to spare a few hundred people in Washington the political inconvenience of having to say no to one influence group or another."[3] The U.S. national debt is now larger than the debts of all the developing countries of Asia, Africa, and Latin America combined.[4] The chief economist at the International Monetary Fund (IMF) said in 2003 that if a developing country had the fiscal record of the United States today, he would be "pretty concerned." An IMF report in January 2004 warned that the growing U.S. debt threatened global economic stability.[5] The Reagan-era deficits that swelled the national debt hardly got paid down at all in the brief four years of Clinton surpluses, and now it's off to the races again.

A 2004 analysis by Brookings Institution economists Alice Rivlin and Isabel Sawhill concluded that under most-likely conditions, the next decade would see the national debt rise from today's $7 trillion to more than $12 trillion. "The interest on this extra borrowing will cost the average household $3,000 a year, and the economic effects of the deficits will also lower its income an estimated $1,800."[6]

The increase in war-related spending is not a small factor in the increasing national debt, and debt is a major source of funding for the new war spending. Again, war is one of three roughly equal reasons for current deficit spending, along with tax cuts and reduced revenue owing to the recession. Economic columnist Jeff Madrick warned in April 2003 that the costs of Iraqi occupation and reconstruction could run into hundreds of billions of dollars in the coming years, creating a "time bomb" for the federal budget. Fareed Zakaria in early 2004 warned that "the mounting federal budget deficits . . . will mean—if history is any guide—sharp cutbacks in American military and foreign-affairs spending. We will see a forced retreat of America's foreign policy similar to the years after the Vietnam War."[7]

Furthermore, as America has gone deeper into debt in recent years, we sell a larger proportion of that debt to foreigners. Economic historian Niall Ferguson cautions that the U.S. position as the world's largest debtor, hooked on foreign capital to

stay afloat, undermines its status as the world's superpower.[8]
David P. Bowers, Merrill Lynch's chief global investment
strategist, said in 2003 that "America is more dependent on the
rest of the world for capital than at any time in the past 50
years." Yet three years ago foreign investors "were being asked
to fund a private sector miracle [sustained growth in the
1990s]. Now they're being asked to fund Bush's tax cuts and
the war in Iraq." The "geopolitical change" in U.S. relations
with traditional allies also "could spell trouble for the funding
of the U.S. economy," said Bowers. "The bottom line is that if
you are a net debtor to the rest of the world, ultimately you
have to be multilateral." But you also have to be activist, the
president of Nomura Securities International said: "Lack of
United States and allied resolve in combating the war on terrorism, and allowing the uncertainties and risks to continue to
weigh on investors' minds . . . is not an answer. We can't survive in the long term without fighting back this enemy."[9]

Which side is right about the deficit? Let's look at Jane Q.
Smith's share of the national debt a bit more closely. The annual budget deficit is the rate of increase in her debt each year.
But this matters only in the context of the size of existing
debts and the interest payments on them. The average household's share of the national debt itself is around $65,000 in
early 2004. (That number has recently surpassed the average
mortgage debt per household.) The government pays around 5
percent a year interest on the national debt—better terms than
Jane Smith pays on her credit cards, more like her home mortgage. But she's adding $6,000 a year to her $65,000.

What Jane Smith cares about this month is not so much her
debt level or how fast it is increasing as the interest payments
due this month. That's the number that can tell us if Jane is
over her limit or still able to handle her situation financially.
The interest payments to service the national debt are around

Box 6   Servicing the national debt, 2004.

Federal on-budget deficit (increase in national debt) per household:
$500/month

Interest paid on national debt per household:
$275/month and rising

$275 per household monthly, meaning that more than half the money Jane borrows each month pays the interest on her past debts (Box 6).[10] These payments will rise in the coming years as the debt increases. But still, Jane can pay the $275 monthly interest, if her income holds up. Even if interest went up to, say, $350 a month, she could pay for the whole thing with the $500 magic-money check and still have $150 left to spend.

Retirement Trust Funds

Actually, Jane Smith doesn't borrow the whole $500 on the credit card each month. She takes about $150 of it from part of the money that goes into her retirement account monthly. She tells herself the money will still be there when she retires, and her retirement plan depends on it. In all, of Jane's household's $65,000 share of the national debt, she owes about $25,000 of it to the retirement plan. Only $40,000 is owed to other people or institutions. Meanwhile, she does pay interest to the retirement plan for what she borrowed. Something like $125 of the $275 Jane pays in interest monthly goes to her own retirement plan. Since she pays this interest to herself, Jane figures that her interest payments are really only $150 a month, not $275. Like the government, she uses a "unified budget" in which the surpluses building up in her retirement plan are counted as reductions in today's spending. This is a fine accounting method until Jane retires.

Jane's "retirement plan" is actually the Social Security and Medicare trust funds. They are producing a surplus these days, while lots of baby boomers are working—and paying payroll taxes—and fewer older people are drawing benefits. But when Jane hits retirement age, the surplus in those funds will turn to a deficit, and the accumulated surplus will be needed for a couple of decades to keep the system solvent with the big payout of benefits to the large retired population. The baby boomers will begin drawing benefits from the trust funds in 2008, gradually fill up the retirement generation over twenty years, and then run it out of money in another fourteen years. Social Security is projected to run out of money and have to reduce benefits in 2042 and Medicare in 2019.[11]

The problems of Social Security and Medicare were brewing long before the current war. The budget was under strain before the War on Terror because of the aging baby boomers, the tax-cutting frenzy, and the sagging economy. The war, again, just makes things worse, because it drives up the deficits.

The Generation Gap

The budget deficit and national debt raise serious issues about equity in our society. The gap between the rich and poor, discussed earlier regarding taxes and budget cuts, is not the only such equity question. There is also what the Concord Coalition calls "generational equity." We are passing on the costs of war, and of tax cuts, to our children and grandchildren, even while undermining the retirement and health funds they will need decades from now. War costs are but one reason that the coming generation gap may be a Grand Canyon.

Think about the sixty million American children in preschool through high school. As we have lowered taxes without lowering expenditures, we have shifted the taxes from ourselves to these children. Meanwhile, we have cut their schools' budgets even though they need more education than ever—and far more language training than we give them—to compete in the globalized economy. High school students will face dramatically higher tuition and fees at state colleges and universities than today's adults paid as college students. In their working lives, today's kids will pay higher payroll taxes to support today's baby boomers after the latter's retirement. Their taxes will be higher too because of paying interest on debts left from the War on Terror. (It would be unconscionable also to leave them the war, unfinished.)

Economists discount the future. The "Popeye" cartoon character Wimpy would "gladly pay you Tuesday for a hamburger today." Money on Tuesday is not worth as much as money today, nor is a hamburger in the future worth as much as one in hand. Economists apply a "discount rate" to future points in time—the further in the future, the less something is worth. For example, if the future is discounted by 5 percent a year, then the promise of a dollar bill a year from now is worth only ninety-five cents today. The promise of a dollar ten years from now is worth only about sixty cents today. That's if you're confident you will be paid then. Uncertainty or risk about getting money back requires a further discount.

The future is an elusive concept to focus our national attention on when our capitalist economy values quarterly earnings reports and our interest-group democracy looks only to the next election. Our children don't get to vote in that election.

The real future is what's out beyond the next earnings report and the next election. Out there in the future, our children and grandchildren will grapple with heavy debts and bankrupt retirement plans. They will have to carry on this country and this planet in whatever shape we leave it to them, as best they can.

The further into the future you look—say, a generation or two—the less value economists will attach to anything. Keynes famously quipped that "in the long run we are all dead."[12] But isn't the idea not just to live until we die but to leave descendants who will carry on our traditions, memories, and genes into the future? To make today's sixty million U.S. schoolchildren pay for today's war is not right. Surely they will have their own wars and struggles, as we have ours.

Past Wars, Past Debts

Still, going into debt in the short term to help pay for war is not the exception but the rule, both historically and across different countries. Access to credit was an important element of military success throughout the wars of Europe's great powers, and played an especially important role in Britain's success in the eighteenth and nineteenth centuries. At a time of need, in wartime, most governments do turn to borrowed funds to help sustain them in the short term. This is entirely appropriate, as even fiscal conservatives agree. But war debts can remain unpaid for years after wars end, undermining the borrower's postwar position and slowing long-term growth.

Consider the advice of the ancient Chinese strategist Sun Tzu, in one of the first books ever written, *The Art of War*, around 400 BC. He told the princes of his time how to use military power to survive and prosper in a dangerous era. War, he wrote, is "a matter of vital importance . . . the road to survival or ruin."[13]

Sun Tzu paid particular attention to the economics of war. Raising an army to attack your neighbor is very expensive. Taking the war to the enemy's territory can reduce the cost somewhat (living off the other's land where possible and keeping destruction off your own land), but this does not eliminate the problem. Throughout Sun Tzu's approach runs a rational cost-benefit calculus familiar to us today.

Sun Tzu believed in paying for war by cash-on-delivery. In Sun Tzu's time, a military campaign required one thousand four-horse chariots, one thousand four-horse wagons, and one hundred thousand troops. All this cost one thousand pieces of gold per day, wrote Sun Tzu. "After this money is in hand, one hundred thousand troops may be raised."[14]

President Bush did it the other way around: first raise the troops and fight the war, then figure out how to pay off the debts. He is hardly the first leader in history to have this idea. For example, in the incessant wars between France and Hapsburg Spain in the sixteenth century, the Spanish king heard from his advisers that three things were needed to wage war: money, money, and more money! Money was also popularly called the "nerves of war" in that century. Historian Fernand Braudel writes that because of rapid advances in military technology—parallel in some ways to today's—war was "an ever-open abyss into which money poured. States of small dimensions went under." States of large dimensions, such as Spain and France, went heavily into debt to pay for war. But the debts caught up with both sides, forced both into national bankruptcy in 1557, and temporarily ended the war. The Spanish bankruptcy caused economic disruption throughout the Hapsburg Empire and has been seen as a key event leading to the decline of Spain's position as a great power. Spain and France became solvent again and went back to fighting, but by 1596, Spain again went bankrupt and "once more brought the mighty Spanish war machine to a halt," in Braudel's words.[15]

As for us, we can only hope that by the time the Bush debts catch up with us, the War on Terror has been definitively won. Stalemate and a century of incessant war would be no better an option for us than it was for the impoverished people of Spain and France in the sixteenth century. As Sun Tzu said, "There has never been a protracted war from which a country has benefited."[16]

The United States has been no exception to the rule of borrowing money for war. As John Steele Gordon details, the U.S. national debt has closely followed war needs from the start, rising during each war and usually being paid down during peacetime.

In 1792, the Revolutionary War left the new federal government's debt at something like 40 percent of the GDP. With the help of new taxes and rising tariff revenues from a trade boom, the debt was paid down to about 10 percent of GDP by 1811. But meanwhile, the largest and most destructive wars the world had ever seen raged in Europe. At first, the United States, as a neutral trading power, benefited. But by the second decade, trade was devastated and the U.S. government thrown into a financial crisis. The British and French seized American ships and their cargoes by the hundreds. In response, the United States imposed the mother of all trade sanctions—first the 1807 Embargo Act banning international trade altogether, and later a ban just on trade with Britain and France, which were America's largest trading partners. (After Napoleon conquered Spain and seized 250 U.S. ships with their cargoes in Spanish ports, he told the protesting U.S. ambassador that France was just helping to enforce the Embargo Act!) U.S. exports fell more than 80 percent from 1807 to 1808. Smuggling took off. Federal government revenues, which depended heavily on tariffs, were cut by more than half in one year, and the budget deficit exploded.[17]

In terms of their attitude toward the federal government and budget, today's Republican leaders resemble the Democratic-Republicans of that time, followers of Thomas Jefferson. They wanted the federal government off our backs, and they thought taxes were *your* money—well, maybe your state's, but not Washington's. Popular opposition to the ruling Federalist Party's tax increases got Jefferson elected president in 1800, and the Democratic-Republicans repealed all the excise taxes. They could afford to cut taxes because, before 1807, the country was at peace, and tariffs alone provided enough revenue.

But that changed as the Napoleonic Wars increasingly affected America. A Western faction known as War Hawks, led by Henry Clay, took over Congress in 1810. In 1811, by a one-vote margin in each house, Congress refused to renew the charter of the U.S. central bank (today's Federal Reserve), whose discipline various state banks resented. Congress declared war against Britain in 1812 on a divided vote, raised army pay, enacted enlistment bonuses, and "then adjourned without raising taxes to pay for the war," writes Gordon. Government spending went from $8 million in 1811 to $20 million in 1812 (and eventually to $34 million in 1814, exceeding revenues by 200 percent). With the country at war, excise taxes were restored but fell far short of the needed revenue.[18]

The anti-Federalist policies of the Democratic-Republicans left war needs desperately underfunded and the military situation dire in 1813. The U.S. Army suffered major defeats in key battles with the British. After nine months at war, writes

Gordon, "the government of the United States, in the midst of a war with a superpower, was dead, flat broke." The government tried to borrow $16 million—much more than ever before—but the drive to sell this debt, which could come into effect only if fully subscribed, stalled at around $6 million. The secretary of the treasury "had less than a week to find the more than $10 million needed to . . . allow the government to operate." He got it from the richest person in the country, Philadelphia banker Stephen Girard, who bought $8 million worth of bonds, reselling $5 million to the public (which trusted him more than it trusted the federal government). In this way the government was able to meet its war costs and turn around the situation on the battlefield, eventually reaching a peace agreement. (Today, covering two months' interest on the national debt would bankrupt Bill Gates.)[19]

The financial rescue of 1813 got the United States through the war, but not before British forces invaded Washington, D.C., and burned the U.S. Capitol, the White House, and most other government buildings to the ground. After 1814, Gordon notes, "Jefferson's political heirs . . . were chastened by the experience of the war" and resurrected a central bank. With the war behind, "the government once again determinedly whittled away at the debt," cutting it by more than half in fifteen years.[20]

The Civil War increased the debt eightfold from 1860 to 1862. It was far more expensive than previous wars—the beginning of an era of mechanized warfare that would culminate in two world wars. During World War I, the debt shot up from 5 percent of GDP in 1917 to 30 percent two years later, even though taxes also jumped, especially income taxes on middle-class Americans. The debt dropped back below 20 percent of GDP in the 1920s, then jumped to over 40 percent during the Great Depression (which lowered tax revenues and raised gov-

Box 7 Debt as a share of GDP.

The U.S. national debt as a share of GDP:

World War II peak: 125 percent of GDP

Vietnam peak: 40 percent of GDP

2003:   60 percent of GDP and rising

ernment spending), and exploded during World War II. The debt was 50 percent of GDP in 1942, and 125 percent in 1945. Obviously, each major war triggered a huge surge of borrowing to meet its costs. Smaller wars have much less dramatic effects. Debt as a share of GDP continued to fall, right through the Korea and Vietnam conflicts, going below 35 percent before the Reagan-era deficits drove debt back up. But by 2003 it was back above 60 percent of GDP and climbing, now propelled by tax cuts, war costs, and an unsteady economy (see Box 7).[21] History demonstrates the natural tendency to rely on debt in wartime, but also the dangers of borrowing too much.

In sum, interest payments to service the national debt, already $275 per household monthly, will rise sharply for years to come. Running up debts in wartime is not unusual but contributes to longer-term problems, notably inflation. The current high deficits might be sustained for several years, but not long term, especially if the War on Terror drags on.

Part Two

BROADER ECONOMIC EFFECTS

It is very important to concentrate on hitting the
U.S. economy through all possible means.

—Osama bin Laden, December 2001

Chapter Five

INFLATION

In addition to government war spending, budget cuts, and debt, other hidden costs of war take their toll. Wartime conditions disrupt economic growth and affect financial markets, commodity prices, investment patterns, and unemployment in complex ways that are more negative than positive overall. Historically, inflation is the biggest of these negatives. Costs of war are also passed along to individual citizens who work harder and make sacrifices without adequate financial compensation. Life in wartime is hard in ways that do not carry a monetary price tag but are very real nonetheless.

The real price of war—the fourth and largest nested box mentioned in Chapter 1—is what we as Americans pay for the whole system that is supposed to give us security against external threats. The $500 a month you pay at the meter in your living room covers only government spending. Off meter, other hidden costs of war erode the economy and reduce the average household's standard of living. Most households lose out economically in wartime, above and beyond the increased government military spending.

History of War-Induced Inflation

The number-one historical effect of war on economics is to create inflation, which lowers the standard of living (see Box 8).[1] The War on Terror will probably cause modestly higher inflation in the coming years.

Historically, inflation is the inevitable consequence of war. It is a form of war "tax" that is most politically palatable and quickest to collect. As governments print or borrow extra money to pay for war, inflation picks up, usually peaking several years after the peak of fighting. A generation of Americans has grown up without firsthand experience of serious inflation, which was tamed here in 1981. But historically, inflation abates between wars and returns with a vengeance when big wars occur. Economic historian Earl J. Hamilton wrote: "Wars . . . without taxation to cover the cost have been the principal causes of hyperinflation in industrial countries in the last two centuries." He blamed the inflation of the 1970s on the Vietnam War and "the unwillingness of our political leaders in both parties to attempt to pay the cost of the war through taxation." Hamilton finds that "of all forms of de facto taxation, inflation is the easiest to levy, the quickest to materialize, and the hardest to evade."[2]

Wartime puts upward pressure on prices across the economy because war destroys the capital needed to make new goods, reducing the supply of some products, while it simultaneously

Box 8 War-induced inflation is an old story.

> "Where the army is, prices are high; when prices rise the wealth of the people is exhausted."
> —Sun Tzu, *The Art of War*, ca. 400 BC

increases demand as the government wades into commercial marketplaces to procure the goods and services needed to prosecute the war. Inflation has distributional consequences. Unlike income taxes, which take more proportionally from the rich than from the poor, inflation hits the poor and middle class hardest.

Because Americans have little experience with very high inflation, let's start elsewhere, with how bad it *can* get. In Angola in the 1980s and 1990s, during a decades-long civil war, people stopped using the government's money and began to value transactions in things like bottles of beer—tangible goods of reliable value. The smart traveler arriving at the airport in the Angolan capital of Luanda in the 1990s did not exchange dollars for Angolan kwanzas, the national currency. The original kwanza was replaced in 1990 by the "new kwanza" with currency controls, in turn replaced in 1995 by the "readjusted kwanza" at one-thousandth the value, in turn replaced in 1999 by a new kwanza at one-millionth of the readjusted kwanza (and thus one-billionth of its original namesake of nine years earlier). So when you got to the airport, you didn't trade dollars for kwanzas. Nobody in the city wanted kwanzas. What people in Luanda wanted was eggs. So you used your dollars to buy flats of eggs, with which you could buy things in the city.[3]

Such hyperinflation commonly follows big wars that devastate a national economy. Hyperinflation can also occur without war; currencies melt down for other reasons. But, historically, wars have caused the worst cases. German hyperinflation after World War I was epitomized by the image of a person pushing a wheelbarrow of cash to buy a loaf of bread. Historian Carroll Quigley said that at the outset of World War I, military leaders in Europe expected a six-month war: "Financial experts . . . while greatly underestimating the cost of fighting, were confident that the financial resources of all states would be exhausted in six months." But instead of this depletion ending the war, it simply made the belligerents break from the gold standard and, in effect, tax their national economies through inflation, according to historian Earl Hamilton.[4]

The expense of World War I did not take everyone by surprise. Writer Jean de Bloch in 1899 argued that the rising costs of war made fighting one "an economic impossibility" that would "result in suicide" if attempted. Author Norman Angell, who later won the Nobel Peace Prize in 1933, said much the same right up to 1914.[5] Both writers thought the disastrous economic consequences would prevent a Great War from taking place, but the war happened anyway. Wars are not about making money, they are about spending money—down to the last dime and beyond, if that's what it takes. Because governments cannot afford to stop spending money in wartime—even when they run out of money—wars produce inflation.

U.S. history shows a pattern of inflation during and after big wars, but at far lower levels than in cases like Angola's. During the U.S. Civil War, both North and South—but especially the South, with its more limited ability to borrow—turned to printing paper money in ever greater amounts. The South suffered from paying more than half its bills with paper money, according to John Steele Gordon: "The effect of this flood of printing-press money on the Southern economy was catastrophic," with 700 percent inflation over the first two years of the war. Meanwhile, inflation totaled 75 percent over four years in the North, driving down real wages (adjusted for purchasing power) by 20 percent, according to historian Roger Ransom. Union-issued "greenbacks" were legal tender but were not accepted even by the government for payment of taxes, Gordon notes. Just as in 2002 the stock market fell or rose on the likelihood of a war in Iraq, during the Civil War "the value of the greenback in terms of gold gyrated in response to Union victories and defeats." (After the war, "cheap money" like the greenback was retained, partly because its inflationary qualities helped debtors. But creditors returned the country to the gold standard by 1879.)[6]

We have government statistics on prices since World War I. The government's Bureau of Labor Statistics creates the urban Consumer Price Index—the most commonly used measure of inflation. You can use the bureau's inflation calculator on the Web at http://data.bls.gov/cgi-bin/cpicalc.pl to see what money from an earlier year is worth in today's dollars. Using this inflation calculator, you can see that the dollar was worth $18.19, in today's terms, in 1915, when Woodrow Wilson was appealing for tax increases for an American military buildup early in World War I. But in 1920, two years after the war ended, the dollar was worth $9.18—a loss of half the dollar's value in five years. The money in your pocket that had bought you two loaves of bread in 1915 got you only one loaf in 1920. Between the world wars, from 1920 to 1941, the dollar's value rose ($9.18 to $12.50). But that 1941 dollar, worth $12.50 in today's (2003) money, became a 1947 dollar worth only $8.24. Thus in six years, during and after World War II, the dollar lost one-third of its value.

After World War II, the U.S. economy never fully returned to peacetime. The Cold War years kept the economy partially in war mode all the time, making low-level inflation a way of life. Still, after a spike of inflation (8 percent) in 1951 during the Korean War, the inflation rate was below 2 percent in twelve of the next fourteen years. The Vietnam War drove annual inflation up to 3 percent in 1966 and 1967, then 4 to 5 percent from 1966 to 1971.

Ever since, inflation rates have been driven by world oil prices, in turn driven by wars and revolutions in the Middle East that affect the prospects for stable future oil exports from that region. Inflation spiked at about 10 percent in 1974 after the Arab oil embargo and Yom Kippur War in late 1973, and again from 1979 to 1981 after the revolution in Iran replaced the U.S.-backed government with an Islamic republic. The inflation rate dropped back from these peaks as world oil prices fell during the 1980s. Overall, the U.S. inflation rate was between 3 and 5 percent in sixteen of the twenty-six years from 1966 to 1991. After the 1991 Gulf War brought expectations of reliable Middle East oil supplies, and after the Cold War ended and military spending fell—eventually by about one-third in the 1990s—inflation dropped back under 3 percent, edging down to 2 percent by 2003.

It is easy to get used to 2 percent inflation. It is low enough not to demand much attention, yet just high enough to give the Federal Reserve a margin to keep dangerous deflation from the door. The last time we had low inflation like this, year after year between 1 and 2 percent, was the early 1960s (see Box 9).[7] Then something happened: inflation jumped to 3 percent in 1965 and climbed to nearly 5 percent by 1970. That something was the Vietnam War. So before you get too used to 2 percent inflation, remember that in a war-prone world, it usually doesn't last.

Box 9 We've had low inflation before, until war ended it.

1959	Barbie Doll goes on sale	0.6 percent inflation
1960	Nixon-Kennedy debates	1.8 percent
1961	Beatles' first show	1.0 percent
1962	Cuban Missile Crisis	1.0 percent
1963	March on Washington	1.3 percent
1964	Ford Mustang introduced	1.3 percent
1969	Vietnam War	4.4 percent
1970	Vietnam War	4.8 percent
1971	Vietnam War	4.4 percent

Will the War on Terror Trigger Inflation?

One thing is for sure, although it would be the least of our problems if it happened: A terrorist nuclear attack would have a strong inflationary effect. Obviously there would be tremendous new demand for medical care, housing, construction, and more. At the same time, the supply of everything would be reduced by what was destroyed in the attack. Demand up and supply down means higher prices. It would be an instant version of what has taken years to develop following past wars.

Barring such a catastrophe, inflation resulting from the War on Terror should be much smaller than inflation following the world wars (15 percent a year in 1919 and 1920 and again in 1946 and 1947), since the current war is smaller in scale and the economy much bigger. Perhaps, as in the late 1960s, we could see a jump from 1 percent inflation to 5 percent. The actual increase would depend on many factors.

Deflationary Pressures

Inflation may be restrained by the effects of some sustained *deflationary* pressures in the world economy. The strong growth of international trade—globalization—has brought vast pools of cheap labor into the global marketplace over the past decade, holding down wages in industrialized countries. Of course, if terrorism ends up putting a big dent in world trade—forcing time-consuming and costly security measures that disrupt global production and distribution—then the deflationary pressures of globalization could abruptly reverse.

The last time Americans saw deflation was in the Great Depression, 1929–33. But Japan has been mired in deflation since the mid-1990s, getting caught in a "liquidity trap" when interest rates kept being lowered without stimulating a recovery, until they bottomed out at zero. Such low rates provided no incentive to lend money, which contributed to slower economic growth, lower demand, delayed consumer purchases, and a deflationary spiral by the late 1990s. In spring 2003, U.S. economists worried about the same happening here (and maybe in Germany) a decade behind Japan. In both Japan and the United States, the slump followed a stock market bubble that burst. A Federal Reserve statement in May 2003 laid out its worries about deflation, signaling determination to avoid Japan's fate of doing too little too late. Federal Reserve chief Alan Greenspan alluded to the threat the same month, saying bluntly that "deflation is a possibility." Once deflation becomes a threat, columnist Robert J. Samuelson wrote, the Fed must undertake very strong economic stimulus measures, even at the price of increasing budget deficits.[8] If the deflation threat were our main concern, then the war spending since 9/11 would serve double duty—not only to prosecute the War on Terror but also to apply war's inherently inflationary pressures as an antidote to possible deflation. In that case the deficit would be less alarming, at least in the short term.

Inflationary Pressures

But other economists in early 2003 found the deflation threat overblown. Jim Paulsen, chief investment strategist for Wells Capital Management, warned of coming inflation in a February 2003 newsletter. "If an economic recovery takes hold," he wrote, "all the pieces for a major inflation fear and bad bond market are already in place." (A bad bond market is one where the bonds you hold are suddenly worth less because interest rates are now higher than when you bought them.)[9]

While attention in early 2003 focused on the danger of deflation, the danger of inflation several years forward received little attention. Inflation will probably take some years to fully develop, barring a catastrophic attack. Wartime inflation typically hits *after* the peak of war: Prices rose fastest in 1919 and 1920, and again in 1946 and 1947. Despite the pressures of globalization to hold prices down, the deficit funding of the War on Terror raises the likelihood of higher inflation in the coming years. When the U.S. government runs up massive deficits to pay for war—not only shunning tax increases but simultaneously cutting taxes—it sets up what economist Paul Krugman has called a "fiscal train wreck." Krugman argues that in the coming years the government will solve the problem in the "usual" way, "by printing money, both to pay current bills and to inflate away debt." (That is, by printing extra money the government devalues the currency in which its own debts are denominated, so they become easier to pay off.)[10]

Effects of Inflation

Deficits affect interest rates because money follows the law of supply and demand. When the government goes into the market for borrowed money—in ever larger amounts—it competes for the same money that you want to borrow to buy a new home or car, and the same money that your boss wants to borrow to grow the company and hire more people. If the government doesn't have enough buyers for its IOUs, it must pay higher interest in order to attract the money it needs to borrow. And that means you will pay higher interest, too. The money that you want to borrow for your mortgage (or that you already have borrowed, if it's an adjustable-rate mortgage) competes in the marketplace with Uncle Sam. In the last inflationary period, the 1970s, interest rates hit double digits (peaking above 15 percent in 1981). The implications of rising interest rates would be serious, especially if the economy continues to rely on housing refinancing as a source of consumer spending. Rising rates would also seriously increase what the federal government pays to service its huge debt. Jane Q. Smith's interest payments of $275 a month (Box 6 on page 63) could potentially double.

When the 2003 tax cuts were under debate, and deficit estimates were skyrocketing, Alan Greenspan warned Congress that by allowing a large federal deficit, "You will be significantly undercutting the benefits that would be achieved from the tax cuts." New studies had strengthened his view that large budget deficits raise interest rates. Those rates, in turn, raise mortgage and car payments and slow business investment and economic growth generally. In 2004, Greenspan reconciled his deficit concerns with his earlier support for tax cuts by suggesting that Congress cut Social Security and Medicare benefits.[11]

Inflation has various other effects. One of the most serious is that it has a confusing effect on our ability to think about money, including war costs, government budgets, taxes, and personal finances. The problem is that the yardstick we measure everything with—money—is itself changing over time. It is the economic equivalent of the theory of relativity, with no fixed, absolute point of reference in time and space. The difference is that while few of us deal with objects traveling near the speed of light, we all deal with money constantly.

Low inflation can be particularly confounding. Suppose the effects of this relatively small war (by historical standards) show up as a modest increase of a few percentage points a year in the inflation rate. As you pushed a cart down aisle 19 of the local supermarket, you might not even notice that the price of eggs had gone up by a penny. Back in Chapter 2, I said that excise taxes were almost invisible and thus politically beautiful. But low inflation is even more beautiful in this way.

Low inflation may affect each of us only a bit at a time, but spread across hundreds of millions of people, a few percentage points adds up to a lot of money—hundreds of billions of dollars each year. Given the resistance to raising taxes, and today's very high budget deficits, inflation may prove the single most important means of paying for the War on Terror in the long run.

Inflation would reduce real wages (that is, wages adjusted for the rising cost of living), which already fell from 2002 to 2003. Paychecks would not go as far. From early 2002 to early 2003, the real weekly salaries of U.S. workers fell about 1.5 percent, dropping for both high- and low-income workers. Companies including AT&T and Boise Cascade froze salaries—thus reducing real wages—while Eastman Chemical cut wages 3 percent, that is, 4 or 5 percent after accounting for inflation. Unionized workers at several giant corporations, such as the big airlines and Boeing, voted to take bigger pay cuts and reduce health care and pension benefits to save their jobs.[12]

It seems likely that *some* inflation—more than conventional wisdom expects—will result from the War on Terror. Maybe it will just be 3–5 percent inflation, compared with the 2 percent we've become used to. Yet even modest increases in inflation over a number of years can reduce our living standard noticeably. Inflation is corrosive. It eats away at everything—especially middle-class savings, stashed away in bonds and bank accounts for future college and retirement expenses. Inflation nibbles away in the background, almost unnoticeable until it becomes really bad, reducing your savings and lowering your real wages so that you can no longer afford what you used to afford. Those particularly hurt by inflation include people with investments in fixed-rate bonds rather than stocks or inflation-indexed bonds, those with large credit card debt, those with variable-rate mortgages, and those with whole life insurance rather than term insurance. (Paul Krugman wrote in early 2003, "With war looming, it's time to be prepared. So last week I switched to a fixed-interest mortgage.")[13]

Fall of the Dollar

As investors decided they preferred other currencies such as the euro to the war-stressed dollar, the value of the dollar relative to those currencies dropped in 2002 and 2003 (Box 10). This helped U.S. exporters but hurt importers and consumers, making a range of imported goods more expensive. And since Americans import much more than we export, it increased inflationary pressures. Trade expert Clyde Prestowitz Jr. wrote in March 2003 that the trade imbalance had been sustained for many years on foreigners' willingness to invest in the United

Box 10 Fall of the dollar during the War on Terror.

Value of one dollar in euros, September 10, 2001:
€1.11
Value of one dollar in euros, February 1, 2004:
€.80 (down 28%)

States. Although war makes the government borrow even more, between 2002 and 2003 foreigners became less interested in investing here. "U.S. international debt is getting so large, foreigners become nervous about their holdings and cut back on buying" government debt, wrote Prestowitz. Low interest rates, which are supposed to help stimulate economic growth, also make the United States a less attractive place for foreigners to invest. So they have been shifting to Europe and Asia. As a result, from 2002 to 2003 the dollar lost a quarter of its value against the euro.[14] War was not the central cause of the dollar's decline, but it contributed to it because increased war spending helped drive up the federal deficit.

In conclusion, the number-one economic effect of war throughout history is to create inflation, reducing the standard of living. Wartime inflation typically follows after a war, as when prices rose 30 percent in just two years in 1919–20 and again in 1946–47. If the coming years see a modest return of inflation, Americans will end up paying for the war in their lower real wages for years to come.

Chapter Six

BUSINESS UNDER STRESS

A kind of shock wave moves through the economy from war fighting. It brings disruption and recession as it goes, and usually ends in inflation several years later. (Similar waves of disruption affect social and cultural life in wartime.) If you have the idea that war's indirect economic effects are good for the economy, compensating for the costs of government spending, forget it. Yes, there are some winners, as Chapter 7 will describe. But there are more losers.

Going back to World War I, the Carnegie Endowment for International Peace estimated the war's overall cost at $400 billion, an amount five times greater than everything of value in France and Belgium then. French industrial production dropped in half from 1913 to 1919, according to Angus Maddison's historical economic statistics. And the blockade of German food imports killed eight hundred thousand civilians, reports historian Carroll Quigley.[1]

The myth arose after World War II that "war is good for the economy" because the war effort seemed to help pull the United States out of the Great Depression of the 1930s. It is true that during periods of great idle capacity, such as the Great Depression, a positive stimulation can result from increased government spending and government control of the economy. But Americans suffered plenty of economic hardships during World War II, and the economy was already growing steadily years before the country entered the war, and returned to the same growth curve after the war. As for the women who gained new economic opportunities working in war jobs, those opportunities also came at a high cost. The women faced grimy, deafening conditions in factories; they still bore the burden of maintaining households and raising children, especially if a husband was away; and after the war, they saw most of their "new opportunities" disappear.[2]

Our last major, years-long war—Vietnam—was not good for the economy. The war undermined the social programs aimed at alleviating poverty in America—President Lyndon Johnson's Great Society. During the final years of the war, and for years afterward, shocked by oil price increases, the economy sank into "stagflation"—a sickly combination of stagnant economic growth and double-digit inflation that eroded American middle-class standards of living.

When the Cold War finally ended and we enjoyed our most peaceful decade in generations—the 1990s—the economy took off. We enjoyed sustained improvement in living standards at all levels of society. Notwithstanding the dotcom investment bubble, information technology and international trade did bring down costs of production all through the global economy, benefiting from a stable international order and reduced military spending. Federal budget deficits turned into surpluses. But now we are back at war and our economy is again shaky. Our surpluses have turned back to deficits, and our standard of living is at risk. No, war is not good for the economy.

Business Expenses

This war puts innumerable burdens on business, many of which are costs paid as part of the war effort or in response to wartime requirements but never accounted for in the statistics of war. In terms of the parking meter in your living room, these costs are not included. The parking meter covers only government spending. These burdens on business illustrate why war is bad for the economy and why most of Big Business does not like wartime.

Let's say you work in an office building in a big city. If the city is New York, you cannot just walk in and go up to your floor. Since 9/11, you have to go through ID checks and security procedures. These are both an inconvenience to workers and an expense to companies, the building's tenants. Under terms of their leases, the companies have to pay the higher costs of added building security, most of which have gone to pay security guards. Outside New York, fewer companies want to pay. If your big city is not New York but Dallas or Los Angeles, the chances are that you *can* walk right into your building, because building tenants have pressured building managers to keep costs low. A survey of twenty-three hundred private commercial buildings nationwide found that security costs rose 14 percent, from forty-nine cents a square foot in 2001 to fifty-six cents in 2002, according to the Building Owners and Managers Association. Todd H. Richardson, managing director of a company that controls thirty-four million square feet of office space in Los Angeles, said that most landlords would not pay more for better security guards. "The smart landlords are focusing on the quality of their security force, but I would say the lion's share have forgotten. They have gone back to pre-9/11 levels of interest."[3] As with government spending, so with the private, hidden costs of war: it's easy to just wish the costs away. But in one way or another the costs must be paid, in this case not by the government but by private companies leasing office space.

Many U.S. corporations do business overseas. The costs of foreign operations have increased somewhat as a result of the War on Terror. The State Department has formed an Overseas Security Advisory Council of more than two thousand companies, which the department advises regularly on security issues overseas. Members include GM, Citigroup, Time Warner, and Procter & Gamble. Subcouncils for particular countries bring U.S. diplomatic resources to bear in order to help corporations manage their overseas operations. For example, the council responded to the 2002 nightclub bombings in Bali, Indonesia—which killed more than a hundred foreigners—by providing companies with what Colin Powell called "timely assessments of the security environment in Indonesia they needed to make their business decisions."[4]

Corporate travel in general has become more complicated. More than three hundred international corporations have contracted with International SOS, a company that provides medical and evacuation services overseas. The company flew out wounded foreign nationals in a C130 cargo plane after the 2003 hotel bombing in Jakarta, Indonesia. A company executive said, "We're tracking the availability of every single wide-body [jet] worldwide," in case of a major emergency. At many big corporations, travel departments have more work and higher expenses in the wartime environment. They need to track employees' locations and work status more closely, in case of an attack. The travel manager for PeopleSoft explained, "You need to understand your travelers. Are they carrying important information that has to get back to the company? What do they have in their briefcases or laptops?" As a travel industry executive put it, "You can no longer just pat [an employee] on the back and say, 'Have a nice trip, see you when you get back.' That just doesn't work. . . . The question is, 'You got him in there? O.K., what's your Plan B to get him out?" Clearly, corporations have had to foot the bill for a whole layer of new expenses related to security in this wartime period.[5]

Of course, Japan, Europe, and much of the impoverished global South are having an even harder time than Americans in the new wartime business environment. Take Egypt, a key battleground of ideas, and sometimes bullets, between radical Islamicists and a U.S.-allied authoritarian government. One-eighth of the country's economy derives from tourism. At the start of the Iraq war, the chairman of the Egyptian Travel Federation, Elhamy el-Zayat, estimated that direct losses from a short war in Iraq would cost Egypt $2 billion in two months. Hotel occupancy, normally at 70 percent at that time of year, was 20 to 40 percent. "The longer [the war] lasts, the worse it is for tourism here," he said. Meanwhile, Turkey, another vital U.S. ally in the War on Terror, suffered a drop in tourism, a $12-billion-a-year industry there, as the war in Iraq convinced Europeans to cancel vacations in Turkey. The Turkish economy was already in critical condition, and the government had forfeited billions of dollars in hoped-for U.S. aid by deciding not to back the U.S. military operation in Iraq. The anxious months before the war in Iraq also took a toll on Asia's export economies, which include other key battleground states such as Indonesia, Malaysia, Singapore, and the Philippines. Higher oil prices and the weaker dollar hurt those countries.[6]

Foreigners and Americans who use Los Angeles International Airport (LAX) will be paying for war as well. The airport was the target of a previous, thwarted plot, and Al Qaeda does like to come back to missed targets. So the airport is being redesigned, at a projected cost of $10 billion over eleven years, to ban cars from the terminal areas and have passengers check in a mile away. The project will be paid from several sources, not including taxes. Landing fees will be increased, and more income will be drawn from concessions and leases. These costs will generally be passed through to the sixty million passengers a year who use LAX.[7] Again, they do not appear in official statistics of war costs.

Perhaps your interest in LAX lies in the stream of foreign tourists who come through en route to your business in hotels, car rentals, or theme parks. According to the Travel Industry Association of America, international travelers pumped about $100 billion a year into the U.S. economy before 9/11 (about $80 a month per U.S. household). But their numbers dropped by a sixth over the subsequent years (see Box 11).[8] New rules adopted for the War on Terror require personal interviews of U.S. tourist visa applicants in far more cases, but without providing more resources to the embassies and consulates that must process them. As a result, U.S. diplomats in Seoul, South Korea, alone may be forced to cut the number of visas issued from five hundred thousand to two hundred thousand a year, as they move from interviewing one-quarter of applicants to 90 percent. Europeans who do not need visas will require computer-readable passports, and all visitors will be fingerprinted and photographed on arrival. Welcome to the U.S.A.! The tourists who end up not coming to the United States as a result of these new restrictions will leave empty beds in hotels and empty tables at restaurants. The executives of the travel association wrote the administration in mid-2003 seeking relief, "a

Box 11 The War on Terror has cost the travel industry dearly.

Money spent in United States
by international travelers . . .

in 2000: $103 billion

in 2003: $85 billion (down 17%)

balance between homeland security and the economy. The government is trying to do too much too soon with too little."
That leaves too much of the cost on the travel industry, already
hard hit.[9]

Maybe you work not in the travel sector but in the health
care sector. A *New York Times* report in March 2003 found that
"hospitals have invested heavily in preparation for an attack,
but they have been forced to absorb most of the costs." In New
York State, by 2003 hospitals were budgeting hundreds of millions of dollars a year—and rising quickly—on terrorist preparedness.[10] One-third went for computer systems and watching for disease outbreaks that would signal a biological weapon.
Another third paid for facilities, equipment, and supplies, from
decontamination units and backup power generators to protective suits, masks, and stockpiles of medicines. The rest covered
training, additional staff, and hospital security. Who pays for
these costs? They go into the price consumers pay for health
care and health insurance. War thus contributes to the rapid
rise in health care costs nationwide, which in turn drives the
state budget crises.

The book publishing business is similarly affected by the
war. "Book sales just stopped after Sept. 11," said Harper-
Collins's CEO Jane Friedman in early 2003. Book sales in 2002

had been disappointing, and the upcoming war in Iraq promised to drive sales down again. "The effect at the cash registers is going to be considerable. We have done numbers. It will be millions of dollars in lost revenue," said Friedman. Similarly, the advertising world is disrupted by war. The anxious months before the war in Iraq were especially difficult for print, radio, and local television stations. "The business in general is holding its breath," said Mel Berning, a top executive with the MediaVest agency. Advertising industry analyst David B. Doft said: "Why make a decision to go ahead with launching a new campaign or a new product when you can wait a couple of months and play it safe? The caution comes from not wanting your ads to show up on TV next to dead bodies."[11]

Airlines saw their advertising plans disrupted by the 2003 war in Iraq. Delta Air Lines "developed a war contingency plan," marketing executive Carter Etherington told business reporter Stuart Elliott. For instance, ads would run in New York "touting security and technology." American Airlines "put advertising on hiatus to monitor how things evolved," with plans to resume advertising in a few weeks, said a company representative. But Continental's spokesperson explained Continental's opposite decision to maintain its advertising: "The war is having enough of a suppressing effect on bookings and traffic that we didn't need to compound it by making ourselves invisible." JetBlue dropped its ads for two days at the start of the war, then resumed them.[12] These business decisions reflect the complexity of coping with war-related disruptions.

Sometimes the costs of war hit home seemingly at random. John Shepherd of Mauldin, South Carolina, took a hit from the War on Terror in 2003. His import company owned a shipping container full of rugs worth $100,000, en route from China, when the U.S. government banned imports from the Chinese firm that had arranged the rug shipment in China. It turned

out that a different part of that Chinese company had sold
Iran items that we don't want Iran to have. The sanctions took
effect immediately, and U.S. Customs seized the container of
rugs. Under Shepherd's contract with the Chinese, he is liable
for the cost of the goods—meaning, the seizure did not affect
the Chinese company, only the American one. Shepherd had to
figure out how to destroy the rugs at his own expense, store
them in Canada, or send them back to China. Meanwhile, he
had to buy more rugs to replace those seized and send them
by air freight—more expensive than by ship—to fill the orders
he had taken from U.S. retailers. When it all settles out, the
War on Terror will have cost John Shepherd's company probably some tens of thousands of dollars. That's above and beyond what he pays in taxes, and elsewhere, to cover the government's expenses. Other companies took a similar hit from
the new sanctions. The extra burden to them never appears in
statistics of the costs of war, but it's a cost. The company executives told a reporter that they didn't complain about the
added costs because they didn't want to seem unpatriotic. "We
wouldn't do anything to harm the United States," Shepherd
said.[13]

The Threat to Trade

In addition to all these disruptions to business, this war threatens to impede international trade—a key source of economic
growth worldwide. Journalist Fareed Zakaria wrote two months
after 9/11 that the slowdowns at U.S. borders were imposing
large economic costs: "The 1990s were exclusively focused on
openness, speed and accessibility—with huge economic benefits. The Institute for International Economics estimates that

about half of the productivity boom of the late 1990s was created by ease and openness of transportation, communication and distribution—globalization." In a post-9/11 world, Canadian suppliers can no longer make deliveries to U.S. companies six hours after receiving an order. Indeed, a CEO at a large American company told Zakaria, "We spent the 1990s taking redundancies out of the system. We are going to spend the next decade putting them back in." Zakaria concludes, "We must find intelligent ways to combine legitimate security concerns with an open, fast-paced, free-market economy. Otherwise we will have to get used to permanently lower growth rates, decreased standards of living and economic stagnation."[14]

Port security continues to get low-to-failing grades from terrorism experts. Progress is taking place, but slowly. Of particular concern are the nearly twenty thousand seaborne shipping containers per day that enter the United States, only a few percent of which are searched or x-rayed. Al Qaeda's assets include experience with oceangoing cargo shipping, and the group has used seaborne containers to ship weapons and explosives. In the worst case, a nuclear weapon could explode without ever leaving its container, destroying a port and contaminating much of a nearby city. With the American economy heavily dependent on international trade, the loss of a major port would inflict widespread economic pain, though it is hard to estimate in dollar terms. The Congressional Research Service—part of the Library of Congress—analyzed the possibility in a 2002 report, "Terrorist Nuclear Attacks on Seaports: Threat and Response." The report quoted U.S. Customs Commissioner Robert Bonner, who said that after a nuclear attack from a shipping container, "the shipping of sea containers would stop," with "devastating" economic effects worldwide.

The report also notes that "current front-line capability to detect nuclear weapons is exceedingly limited." As one Coast Guard officer wrote, "Our method of detecting nuclear and biological weapons is . . . our eyes, ears, and brains."

The Customs Service in 2003 began putting in place a Container Security Initiative (CSI), which aims to improve security at foreign ports where U.S.-bound containers are loaded—for instance, by installing electronic seals on low-risk shipments, allowing inspectors to concentrate on higher-risk ones. But the Congressional Research Service report pointed out that at foreign ports U.S. officials "do not inspect cargo there and do not control personnel selection or port operations. . . . The Coast Guard cannot open containers at sea for various reasons. . . . Problems are obvious. Terrorists could infiltrate foreign ports as inspectors or longshoremen, and pass a container with a weapon into a secured zone. The Coast Guard almost certainly could not detect a bomb in a container." Furthermore, the report criticizes U.S. Customs for targeting shipments for inspection based on manifest data, port of last call, and so forth, when terrorists "could be expected to go to great lengths to make a bomb-carrying container appear normal." And, of course, "once a ship arrives in port, any inspection could be too late."

The trouble is that imposing security on borders, ports, and containers cuts two ways. True, too little would be a terrible mistake. But too much would also be a mistake, because it would seriously impede trade and add to the costs of doing business worldwide. Beyond the government's additional costs, businesses—and ultimately workers and consumers—would have less chance to prosper.

But so far, it seems the error has been on the side of not spending enough to ensure port security—a recurrent complaint to the federal government by coastal cities. In the first two years the CSI program concentrated on training three

Box 12 The Container Security Initiative (CSI), 2003.

> Number of inspectors being trained to inspect U.S.-bound shipping containers:
> **300**
>
> Number of shipping containers entering the United States each week:
> **135,000**
>
> Inspector's time available for each shipping container on average, including physical inspection, paperwork, meetings, travel time, and bathroom breaks:
> **5 minutes**

hundred inspectors and putting about five inspectors at each of the twenty largest European and Asian ports, none in Muslim countries. Agreements had been reached with nineteen of them, with five "fully operational," according to a March 2003 Customs fact sheet. Expansion into some of the major ports in Muslim countries such as the United Arab Emirates, Malaysia, and Turkey was just being planned. Even after that phase is completed, terrorists will still have many smaller ports in which to place a weapon into a U.S.-bound container. One issue slowing down the program's expansion is that the United States requires the foreign governments to provide the needed x-ray and radiation-detection equipment at their own expense. And even if all three hundred inspectors could stand—full time, with never a sick day—at three hundred assembly lines with inbound containers passing by, they would have but five minutes to devote to each container (see Box 12).[15]

Financial Markets and War Jitters

Financial markets responded negatively to war in the half year leading up to the 2003 Iraq campaign. Investors knew that capitalism thrives on political stability. War is bad for business, and investors who buy into magical thinking or succumb to denial do not last long. For six months before the war in Iraq, stock markets carried on a back-and-forth dance: When an Iraq war seemed more likely, markets fell; when the threat of fighting receded, markets rose. Investors were especially worried that a war could disrupt the oil flow from the Middle East, which would make oil prices rise globally and prolong the world economic downturn. In addition, they feared that the costs of an Iraq war, which some White House officials had estimated at $100 billion or more, would drag down a U.S. economy just starting to recover from an unsettling recession. Worse still, a new war could inflame passions in Muslim countries and might lead to retaliation on U.S. soil, possibly by terrorists using weapons of mass destruction. In short, the price of war loomed large across the economic landscape.[16] Barton Biggs, global strategist for the investment bank Morgan Stanley, expressed enthusiasm for short-term stock market gains in October 2002 but predicted three to five years of "relatively slow growth almost everywhere around the world" because "terrorism is a menace to growth."[17]

In November 2002, as the Bush administration pushed its case for a war in Iraq, it fell to Federal Reserve chairman Alan Greenspan to try to calm fears, sitting in the hot seat under the glare of TV lights at a congressional hearing. As usual, he spoke in even tones, betraying little emotion. A misplaced word, seemingly even a raised eyebrow, could send financial markets into a panic. On this day, Greenspan had particular reason to be careful: investors were skittish and bad economic news was mounting. The economy was hitting a "soft patch," in Greenspan's words. At the top of investors' list of worries was a possible U.S. war against Iraq. Indeed, Greenspan attributed the economy's soft patch to several factors including, "perhaps most importantly, currently the geopolitical risks surrounding the negotiations with Iraq."

But not to worry, Greenspan told the Congress and investors. The economic effects of an Iraq war would be "modest, largely because this is not Vietnam or Korea." The Korean War in the early 1950s, he said, "had a really monumental effect, basically because the economy was so much smaller than it is today." With a larger economy and higher standard of living now, Greenspan said in effect, we could take the hit. Even a war cost of $100 billion would amount to just 1 percent of our GDP.[18]

In truth, nobody knew how much a war would cost, because it depends on how long the fighting lasts, how long U.S. troops occupy Iraq, the costs of reconstruction, whether oil prices rise or decline, and whether retaliation against U.S. targets causes damage elsewhere.[19] The White House economic adviser Lawrence Lindsey, at about the same time as Greenspan's testimony, said that economic prospects were uncertain because the war on terrorism and the war in Iraq "have economic and psychological effects that are very difficult to evaluate and predict." Two months earlier he suggested that the costs of an Iraq war might reach $200 billion, a cost he dismissed as "nothing" compared with the whole U.S. economy.[20] By December Lindsey was out of a job, and the administration avoided giving any more cost estimates until the war was under way. True, as Greenspan said, this impact would be less than Vietnam, Korea, and especially World War II (when 40 percent of GDP

was devoted to the war). But anywhere in the wide range of estimates, we are talking big numbers. As it turned out, $200 bil-
lion was not a bad estimate.

Financial markets dropped immediately after Greenspan's
testimony. His message, that a war would be costly but the cost
could be spread around, was not reassuring to investors
spooked by war and terrorism. Sure, we could take a $100 bil-
lion hit in a $10 trillion economy, but it was still a big hit. And
what about the bigger War on Terror? The year before, the
9/11 attacks had cost perhaps $100 billion, and the next year—
who knows? More wars, against North Korea and Iran? More
terrorist attacks? Already, these dangers were reflected on international currency markets as a "risk discount" associated
with the U.S. dollar (which was to lose nearly 20 percent of its
value against the European currency in the subsequent six
months as the war in Iraq approached).

Markets rebounded later in the day only when wire reports
came in that Iraq had accepted a UN Security Council resolution on weapons inspections, making a war somewhat less
likely. But over the next four months, as the Iraq war drew
closer and closer, the U.S. economy grew weaker and weaker.
The stock market hit new lows, gasoline prices hit new highs,
job losses and layoffs mounted, and airline companies followed
each other into bankruptcy. Nearly all the fifty states grappled
with their worst budget crises in decades, forcing painful cuts.
The dance of financial markets continued right up through the
start of the war in Iraq. On Friday, March 14, when a UN vote
was put off, indicating a war would *not* start the next Monday,
the Dow Jones industrials rose by 3 percent and the Nasdaq by
5 percent.

After the war began, stocks rose and fell on hopes that the
war would end quickly and decisively. On March 23, with U.S.
and British forces charging deep into Iraq, the Dow gained 8

percent in a week. The chief economist at brokerage A.G. Edwards explained that "there was a lot of uncertainty up to this week—concerns about the war, worst-case scenario situations."[21]

Alan Greenspan was not wrong to estimate the costs of an Iraq campaign as "modest" compared with the whole U.S. economy. But this view misses the big picture of the country in a War on Terror of unknown duration, fought in part on U.S. territory, bringing in its train major hikes in military spending at a time of high national deficits. The cost of this insecurity on people's lives and productivity is very high. In fairness, Greenspan's job is to calm markets, not to sound an alarm about risks that investors are well aware of already. And by February 2003, Greenspan was pretty direct—for him—in telling the Senate that war jitters were holding back economic recovery: "The heightening of geopolitical tensions has only added to the marked uncertainties that have piled up over the past three years, creating formidable barriers to new investment and thus to a resumption of vigorous expansion of overall economic activity."[22]

War anxiety restrains both spending and investment, which slows growth. In a *USA Today*/CNN/Gallup poll six weeks before the Iraq war began, one-quarter of consumers said they were cutting back on spending because of the threat of war. "You hate to go ahead with very much because you don't know what is going on," Gail Briner of Wayzata, Minnesota, told *USA Today*. At age sixty-one, she worried about how war might affect her already depressed stock portfolio. Meanwhile, at his marketing firm in St. Louis, Keith Alper delayed purchasing a new color copier and laser printer, saying, "We need them, but they're not an immediate need. We're waiting for the war." His clients, large companies, were delaying product launches and large staff meetings because they expected war to

disrupt travel.[23] Such is the psychology of wartime. Rising unemployment amplified this anxious psychology.

Swift victory in Iraq and falling oil prices were supposed to
rouse the American economy from its wartime slump. They
did not. Business investment stayed restrained, and job losses
mounted. As the chief economist at Standard and Poor's put
it, "We had this big cloud in front of us called Iraq. But we're
still not sure what smaller ones are behind it."[24] A month
later, car bombs killed dozens of foreigners in Saudi Arabia
and Morocco, proving that Al Qaeda was alive and well, and
Iraq had turned into an expensive long-term reconstruction
effort. In April 2003, the U.S.-Asia chief executive of Europe's
largest venture capital firm said: "The American administration has made it clear that they wish to take that battle to
more than just Iraq. My working assumption is that there
will be other events. . . . You'd be foolish to think it would
have no impact on economics."[25] Meanwhile, Iraq itself proved
more costly than expected, and Iraqi oil seemed likely to take
years to return fully to the world market. So world oil prices
stayed relatively high, and U.S. job losses continued, although
stock markets rose robustly in the wake of the war and rapid
GDP growth followed. Thus, notwithstanding any economic
upturn in election year, the shadow of war remains over the
economy. Indeed, it remains over the world economy as a
whole.[26]

Readiness Fatigue

Even without an actual terrorist attack, waiting for one takes
its toll on the national psyche, and hence on business and consumer confidence. In a national poll by University of Maryland
researchers in September 2003, three-quarters of Americans

said they had not come to feel any safer over the two years since 9/11.[27] Similarly, a *New York Times* poll the same month found that 68 percent of New Yorkers were "personally very concerned about another terrorist attack," down only six points from October 2001. One-third of the city's residents said they still "feel nervous or edgy because of Sept. 11," and the same number said their lives had never gotten back to normal. More than half considered another terrorist attack in the United States in the next few months "likely."[28]

The government's color-coded terrorist alerts contribute to our anxiety. If you find them unclear, you're not alone. This is how Jay Leno described them: "This thing is so confusing. Yesterday the alert went from blue to pink; now half the country thinks we're pregnant." Tom Ridge, secretary of Homeland Security and controller of the color alerts, became the frequent butt of jokes on late-night TV. But Ridge had the last laugh. Appearing on the *Tonight Show,* Ridge was asked by Leno, "I'm sitting at home in my underpants watching the game and, boop, we're in yellow. What do I do now?" Ridge's unscripted response: "Change shorts."[29]

The question remains, though: What are we supposed to do? A 2003 report by the nonpartisan Congressional Research Service noted that the "vagueness" of warnings "raised concerns that the public may begin to question the authenticity of the . . . threat level." Psychologist Philip Zimbardo, in early 2003, concluded that the terror alerts violate basic principles of psychology and common sense. The government gives out vague information—everyone be on the lookout everywhere for something—but tells citizens to go about normal business. Then alerts are lifted without explanation of why nothing happened, leading to a boy-who-cried-wolf reaction. When the government put out a program for the public to follow—online at www.ready.gov—Zimbardo found the same problems as with earlier terror alerts: "mixed, confusing actions recommended." For instance, in the event of a chemical attack, first "take immediate action to get away," then "staying put and avoiding uncertainty outside" is recommended. Zimbardo adds, "Go–Stay? Which way?" Zimbardo thinks that living on constant alert against undefined dangers creates what he calls "pre-traumatic stress syndrome" and a "heightened sense of anxiety and confusion" in the American public.[30]

In summary, wartime conditions disrupt economic life, including financial markets, commodity prices, investment patterns, and unemployment. Business, especially global business, does best in peace and suffers in wartime.

Chapter Seven

PROFIT AND LOSS IN WARTIME

Although war is a net economic loss, not everyone wins and loses equally. Some people benefit economically from wars while others—the majority—suffer economic losses. And some of the latter suffer bigger losses than others. Whole sectors of the economy can prosper or wither as a result of wartime changes. In this war, for example, not every company suffers from the general problems discussed in Chapter 6. Defense contractors make big profits while airlines take big losses. Let's look at the profiteers first. Individuals, companies, and whole industries can prosper in wartime, depending on conditions. War shakes up societies, sending some up and some down. The government can also direct military spending to particular locations or companies, advancing them economically.

Defense Contractors

On the whole, peacetime is far better for making money in this globalized era than is wartime. One sector, however, is the exception: those who sell goods and services for the war.

Military contractors and suppliers, including arms makers and others whose goods are needed in wartime, benefit from war. During active fighting or heightened defense preparation—including the current period since 9/11—these companies have higher revenue and higher profits. For example, the Raytheon company of Lexington, Massachusetts, produces the Tomahawk cruise missile, hundreds of which were fired in the early days of the war in Iraq. In 2002, Raytheon completed a batch of more than six hundred Tomahawks, and in 2001–3 the company was retrofitting four hundred more with global positioning system (GPS) navigation, at more than half a million dollars apiece. The company announced early in 2003 that it would accelerate production of the missiles. In the next six years, the U.S. Navy plans to buy thousands more—probably a billion-dollar order—with an even better navigation system that will allow mid-flight retargeting. Defense analyst Robert C. Martinage called the Tomahawk's performance in the Iraq war "good news for Raytheon."[1]

The War on Terror was also good news for General Atomics Aeronautical, which makes the Predator unmanned plane, used for surveillance and fitted with Hellfire missiles for use against terrorists in Afghanistan and elsewhere. The Pentagon in 2003 doubled its spending on such unmanned aircraft. The war has also boosted the fortunes of smaller companies lucky enough to produce goods suddenly in demand. For example, L-3 Communications, a New York company that makes equipment to scan baggage and shipping containers for explosives, had a 50 percent rise in its stock price in the two years after 9/11.

Similarly, Boeing tripled production of satellite guidance kits for smart bombs, projecting $5 billion in Pentagon orders for the highly profitable systems by 2010. However, since the war in Iraq was fought with the existing inventory of weapons, with spares ordered as needed, it was not a boon for defense factories. It may have even diverted funds that would otherwise have paid for new weapons but were instead needed to send troops and equipment to the Middle East. Boeing CEO Phil Condit warned that "money getting spent to fight a war then is not getting spent on future programs," such as Boeing's next-generation unmanned bomber—programs that matter to Boeing much more than making guidance systems for bombs.[2]

More broadly, from early 2002 to early 2003, orders for military capital goods rose by one-quarter, even though factory orders in the civilian economy dropped as business investment was held back by prewar fears. In the last quarter of 2002, higher military spending accounted for nearly two-thirds of the sluggish GDP growth of below 1 percent. So this period was good to the defense sector. The war in Iraq itself was not expected to be a huge boost to the sector, because by historical standards it was small-scale. But the rising trend of defense spending in recent years gives all these companies a boost.

Beyond the arms manufacturers, a whole range of companies making products useful in wartime stand to profit in the new wartime period. For instance, the 2003 war in Iraq generated a big demand for training and equipment for international journalists covering the conflict. Training courses in Britain and the United States on how to handle a hostile environment had a surge of enrollments, at several thousand dollars per participant. At the British company Centurion Risk Assessment Services, which offers such training, business doubled from early 2002 to early 2003. Sales of satellite phones increased. And at the British company Expedition Kit Limited—purveyor of bulletproof vests and other combat accessories (as well as mundane camping gear)—sales have quadrupled. "It's been absolutely fantastic for business," said cofounder Tim Simpson.[3]

Is it wrong for companies like Raytheon or Expedition Kit to profit from war? The country is at war, it needs cruise missiles, and Raytheon makes them. Being able to make cruise missiles is a strength of the American economy, which will contribute to winning the war.

But it's another matter if some companies make mega-profits because of political cronyism, campaign contributions, and the like—rather than because they make the best missiles. President Dwight Eisenhower famously warned, in his farewell address, of a "military-industrial complex" that was becoming too powerful for our fragile democracy, using political clout to drive up defense spending and therefore profits. Columnist Bob Herbert, in the wake of major combat in Iraq, accused Reagan-era secretary of state George Shultz of promoting war in Iraq so that the company he once headed and still sits on the board of—engineering giant Bechtel Group of San Francisco—could profit from reconstruction contracts. Shultz headed the prowar Committee for the Liberation of Iraq, and his political connections may have helped (they certainly didn't hurt) Bechtel to win a $700 million, eighteen-month reconstruction contract, with more expected to follow. The contract was awarded without a competitive bidding process. Democratic senator Ron Wyden of Oregon told Herbert, "You look at this process, which is secret, limited, or closed bidding, and you have to ask yourself, 'Why are these companies being picked?'"[4]

Another big winner in the Iraq war was the U.S. company Halliburton. From mid-2002 to mid-2003, Halliburton won approximately $2 billion in U.S. government contracts associated with the war in Iraq, according to a *Washington Post* investigation. The *Post* called the Iraq revenue "a major factor" in Hal-

Box 13 Halliburton's Iraq contracts.

Estimated value of Halliburton's U.S. government
contracts for Iraq, mid-2002 to mid-2003:
$2 billion

Rise in Halliburton stock value, September 2002 to
September 2003:
From $12.55 per share to $24.12 = 92 percent

liburton's stock-price increase during that year (see Box 13).[5]
Some contracts were in Halliburton's original area of spe-
cialty—oil well and pipeline servicing. But most were in an
area Halliburton had focused on in recent years—providing
services to the military that include building and operating
bases, cooking hot meals, and helping with logistics. After the
1991 Gulf War, then–defense secretary Dick Cheney commis-
sioned a Halliburton subsidiary, Brown and Root, to study how
to outsource routine Pentagon operations on a large scale. The
Pentagon then awarded the contract to implement the study's
recommendations to Brown and Root, and Cheney himself became CEO of Halliburton from 1995 to 2000—up to the eve of
his vice presidential campaign—and pushed the company further into a broad range of military service contracts. In the Iraq
war, the *Post* reported, up to one-third of the $4 billion
monthly costs of U.S. operations in Iraq in mid-2003 went to
independent contractors, headed by Halliburton and including
Bechtel for reconstruction work, DynCorp for training Iraqi
police, and other companies.

There is something sleazy about big, politically connected
corporations cashing in with juicy contracts in wartime. But it's

pretty much the same process in peacetime. Maybe the no-bid contracts cost the U.S. taxpayers a little more, but it's all small change in the big picture of war costs. Maybe George Shultz's lobbying made a war in Iraq slightly more likely, and Bechtel made more money as a result; but lots of other powerful interests were lobbying for and against the overthrow of Saddam Hussein and the reconstruction of Iraq. The idea that any one crony can drive U.S. policy or that any president would make major foreign policy decisions based on the parochial interests of any one sector or interest group does not do justice to the complexity of our democracy, even with its flaws. Protesters can march in the streets saying, "No War for Oil," and Shultz can lobby in the corridors of power for the liberation of Iraq. But George W. Bush knows that to stay in power he must look out for a range of interests and constituencies. There is not a conspiracy to run the country for the exclusive benefit of Bechtel or Halliburton, or any other narrow group, company, or sector of the economy.

Also relatively unimportant in the big picture of wartime economics is the favoritism that steered Iraq reconstruction contracts to American companies rather than foreign ones. Perhaps it wasn't fair, but companies from other countries faced a disadvantage in winning contracts. Beyond just Iraq contracts, Canadian executives worried that Canada's lack of support for the U.S. war effort would leave Canadian companies at a disadvantage in dealing with the U.S. government on broader concerns, such as trade disputes. The president of the Canadian Manufacturers and Exporters group told his members during the fighting in Iraq that the group had reminded the Canadian government "that anti-American statements by government officials can have serious consequences for Canada and . . . urged that they stop." A group of ninety Canadian business leaders meanwhile visited Washington, D.C., during the war to patch up relations.[6] But even in Britain, America's closest ally, frustrated company executives met with their government to ask for help winning U.S. contracts for Iraq. Also lobbying were Russian and French companies that had signed billions of dollars of contracts with Saddam Hussein, covering oil exploration and reconstruction after the lifting of UN sanctions.

However unfair, even unseemly, the awarding of war contracts may be, the profiteering of defense companies is a small slice of the big picture of wartime economics. These profits for the few are far smaller than the higher government costs, taxes, deficits, and inflation caused by war and the disruptive effects of war on business. Juicy war contracts are a by-product of war, not its cause. The companies that profit from war are free riders, not the driving force.

Pork Barrel Politics

Defense contractors are not the only beneficiaries of war spending. Consider the March 2003 supplemental appropriation of nearly $80 billion. The bill had to pass, and within weeks, to keep the war going, so members of Congress had a golden opportunity to put in spending provisions for things like homeland security measures, help for the airline industry, the 9/11 commission, and foreign aid. The sequence of *New York Times* headlines says it all: March 25, "Bush Requesting Nearly $75 Billion for War Costs"; March 27, "Hands Out for Shares of War Budget"; April 9, "Senate Rolls a Pork Barrel into War Bill"; April 11, "Money Bill for War Stalls over Alaska Senator's Insistence on Special Interest Extras," with the subheading "The Pentagon warns that it could start running out of money for the war." Ah, democracy in action.

The Alaska senator, Republican Ted Stevens, chair of the Appropriations Committee, included some vital wartime projects such as aid to the Alaskan salmon industry and dams in the home states of committee members. The House of Representatives made him take out fifteen of the twenty extras unrelated to war, but the following provision stayed in the bill as signed into law by President Bush: Alaska salmon caught at sea may now be sold as "organic," overriding the opposite recommendation of an advisory panel to the U.S. Department of Agriculture in 2001. Alaskan salmon, say its backers, is inherently organic because it comes from "pristine" Alaskan oceans. I have no idea which side is right about the organic label on Alaska salmon, but I know it has nothing to do with the important business of funding the War on Terror; nor did Senator Stevens's amendment to the counterterrorism bill a year earlier, adding a $5 million loan program for Alaskan fisheries. Senator John McCain had this reaction: "I knew we were in an emergency here in the country. But these fishing loans for halibut, I guess there is a halibut problem up in Alaska of which, unfortunately, the nation has not been made aware."[7]

Senator Stevens's organic-salmon gambit did not cost the federal budget; it came at the expense of competing producers of farm-grown salmon in other states. But other demands do compete for scarce federal resources. Take Senator Stevens's questioning of the U.S. Coast Guard commandant, Admiral Thomas H. Collins, at a hearing of the Senate Appropriations Committee's Homeland Security Subcommittee on May 1, 2003. According to a press release his office issued on the day of the hearing, just as major combat was ending in Iraq, the senator "expressed concern" to the admiral that he had not assigned enough cutters to patrol Alaskan waters against foreign fishing ships making incursions into Alaskan fishing grounds. Senator Stevens suggested that Predator unmanned aircraft be assigned to patrol Alaskan fishing grounds and warn off poachers. The Predator is a crucial weapon in the War on Terror and in critically short supply because it is what the Pentagon calls a "high demand/low density asset"—a term translated by Secretary of Defense Donald Rumsfeld as "We didn't buy enough." The idea that a scarce and vital military asset could be reassigned from the War on Terror to guard the economic interests of one state, whose senator chairs the Appropriations Committee, boggles the mind.

Corporate America versus Big Oil

In fall 2002, one hundred thousand protesters rallied against the Iraq war in Washington, D.C.—the biggest such rally up to then. The organizers, a coalition called International ANSWER (short for "Act Now to Stop War and End Racism"), argued that the threatened Iraq war "serves only the interests of Big Oil" and shows that "Bush and Congress . . . represent the interests of Corporate America rather than the people of the United States." By attacking Iraq, according to ANSWER, Bush "seeks to conquer the oil, land and resources of the Middle East." (Actually, land and resources are synonymous with oil in this case.) ANSWER saw the war primarily as a grab to control cheap oil so that Corporate America generally, and U.S. oil companies in particular, would be more profitable.[8]

CORPORATE AMERICA

ANSWER's view is demonstrably wrong. Let's look first at the argument about Corporate America benefiting from the war, and then the argument about Big Oil. There is a central contradiction in the claim that the war in Iraq served Corporate

America. Corporate America was against the war! This is clear from the swings of financial markets on investors' *fears* of war, which I described in Chapter 6. Corporate executives' mission is to increase their companies' stock prices, and those prices dropped every time the prospect of Bush's proposed war grew more immediate.

The truth is that Corporate America is most profitable in a stable, peaceful world of free trade. War and military spending undermine those stable, predictable conditions. There are always some companies that profit from wartime, but neither big corporations as a whole nor the U.S. economy as a whole do so. The stock market doesn't lie about Corporate America's interests. Corporate America is antiwar.

One aspect of the war in Iraq that Corporate America *would* like, however, is the idea of lower, more stable world oil prices in the future. Oil—along with other fuels that it more or less can replace—is an absolutely critical input to the Western economies. Every major increase in world oil prices in recent decades has been followed by a recession in the Western industrialized economies. The 2001 recession followed the doubling of oil prices from 1999 to 2000. Oil is the world's most internationally traded commodity in dollar value—and the world oil trade is heavily dependent on exports from the Middle East, and from Saudi Arabia in particular.

If regime change in Iraq ended sanctions, spurred foreign investment in Iraq's oil industry, and thus brought more oil onto world markets—and removed a persistent threat to Saudi Arabia—that could drive down world oil prices, which would be good for the U.S. economy overall and for your heating bill and gas tank. Undersecretary of Commerce Grant Aldonas told a business forum in late 2002 that a war in Iraq "would open up this spigot on Iraqi oil, which certainly would have a profound effect in terms of the performance of the world economy."[9]

Iraq has the world's second largest reserves of crude oil, with about half the amount of the largest, Saudi Arabia. Iraq's oil reserves are five times larger than U.S. reserves. After a decade of UN sanctions, and decades of war before that, all ruled over by a brutal police state, Iraq's oil industry is a mess. Getting up to speed will take years of work and billions of dollars. After that, Iraq will pump a lot of oil, which presumably will lower oil prices over the long run. That will be good for the industrialized economies—and bad for producers such as Saudi Arabia, Mexico, and Nigeria, and for the global environment.

BIG OIL

According to critics like ANSWER, the war benefits Big Oil in particular. It is plausible that the oil sector would receive favorable treatment from the Bush administration, for both political and personal reasons. In the words of an MSNBC report in 2002, Bush, Cheney, and Condoleezza Rice "all claim a stunning pedigree" in the oil business: Bush was a director of Harken Energy, Cheney was CEO of Halliburton, and Rice was on the Chevron board and reportedly holds about $200,000 of Chevron stock in a blind trust. (Chevron even named an oil tanker the *Condoleezza Rice*, but renamed it in 2001 when she joined the Bush administration. Presumably, the picture of the bright red tanker with a huge Chevron logo and her name on the bow would have brought unwanted attention to the administration's close ties with oil companies.) A study by the nonpartisan Center for Public Integrity found that the top one hundred Bush administration officials together held $150 million of investments—that's $1.5 million each on average—with the majority in the energy and natural resources sector.[10]

But the very scenario that Corporate America would welcome—a successful regime change followed by reductions of world oil prices—would hurt Big Oil. Low oil prices, so good for U.S. economic growth, are terrible for oil companies. The big oil companies *sell* oil. Big industrial companies *buy* oil. What's nectar to one is vinegar to the other. Oil industry leaders said in 2003 that a war in Iraq, by freeing vast new reserves and potentially increasing world production, would drive down oil prices and their own profits. Even if Big Oil comes into Iraq and gets a piece of the production there, most of its oil will always be produced elsewhere.

Indeed, one business article in late 2002 advised investors that they could, if they have "a strong stomach for risk," sell short energy stocks in anticipation of a war (meaning, you gamble the stock price will fall). The reasoning was that a quick, successful war would drive down oil prices—which had been staying high because of anxiety about war scenarios that could interfere with the oil trade. Lower oil prices would mean lower oil company profits, which would mean lower stock prices (see Box 14).[11] Indeed, the immediate effect of the war in Iraq, when it came, was to *end* a boom in oil company profits that had resulted from the high oil prices in the months before the war. In the first quarter of 2003, Shell and Chevron-Texaco earnings doubled, and ExxonMobil and BP also posted large gains. When the U.S. victory in Iraq lowered oil prices somewhat, it also lowered Big Oil's profits. And when problems mounted in Iraq and world oil prices rose again later in 2003, oil company profits went up. But the big jump in oil prices—doubling from 1999 to 2000 and helping cause the 2001 recession—was not related to war.

Thus, to the extent that a Corporate America with one set of interests exists, those interests lie in world political stability and security. Corporations make money best under stable and predictable rules and conditions. Beyond that, different corporations have different interests. It's not just that oil prices affect

Box 14 Conflicting interests of oil companies and "Corporate America."

World oil prices rise when political instability in the Middle East threatens supply.

The effects of higher oil prices:

U.S. economic growth—lower
Profits of most U.S. corporations—lower
Oil company profits—higher

Conclusion: Oil companies and Corporate America have opposite interests on this issue.

oil companies and manufacturing industries oppositely. The drop in the U.S. dollar in 2003 hurt importers but helped exporters. A future wave of inflation would help debtors and hurt creditors, and so forth. Seeing war as a gain for Corporate America at the expense of working people is the wrong way to think about the costs of war. The big picture is not that corporations are using war to profit at the expense of ordinary people. Rather, the big picture is that an expensive war harms the economic interests of *both* corporations and ordinary Americans. You can debate corporations versus people, but it won't help you understand war costs.

The Loss Column

While some profit more than average in wartime, others lose more than their share. In addition to the losses suffered by giant corporations and small businesses in wartime—as detailed in Chapters 6 and 7—individual Americans also take economic and noneconomic losses in wartime as well. Soldiers and veterans top this list.

SOLDIERS

Vanessa Turner took a big loss in this war. In August 2003 the war left her sick and homeless, living with her fifteen-year-old daughter on the floor of her sister's friend's one-bedroom apartment in Boston's poor Roxbury neighborhood, where she grew up. Three months earlier Turner had been a sergeant in the U.S. Army in Iraq, a cook who had watched tracer fire while washing pots. She collapsed—possibly from chemical exposure or a reaction to mosquito-bite lotion—and was rushed away by medics, her heartbeat down to twenty and unable to move, though conscious long enough to hear someone say, "This soldier's not going to make it." Evacuated to Germany, Turner was expected to live fewer than three days. She was quickly classified as "medically retired," to expedite death benefits to her daughter. But that meant she was no longer an active-duty soldier, so the U.S. military would not pay for her family to fly to Germany to her bedside. The family couldn't afford airline tickets but got transportation and lodging with the help of the USO and a private foundation.[12]

Turner, a strong woman whose hobbies included weightlifting, survived. After six more weeks of treatment in Washington, D.C., she was sent home to Roxbury with continuing medical problems, including serious nerve damage in one leg. However, she was no longer a service member but suddenly a veteran and was told to wait three months for an initial appointment at the local VA hospital. It took the intervention of her senators to get an earlier appointment. The military initially refused to send her personal possessions home from Iraq and Germany, saying that retrieving them was her responsibility. After seven years in the military's care, she was suddenly out of a home, a job—good luck trying to find one in Roxbury in 2003—and the other necessities of life. Her sister said, "They threw her away like a piece of trash. She served her country and now nothing is being done for her."

A VA official told the Associated Press that Turner's lack of immediate access to VA services was a "mistake" by the VA facility in West Roxbury. But just weeks earlier the Veterans of Foreign Wars (VFW) had expressed "dismay" at proposed congressional funding for veterans' health care, which would *decrease* in inflation-adjusted terms and fall $2 billion short of what had been promised earlier. "The House leadership has deceived us," said the VFW's leader Ray Sisk in a press release. "It is another instance where veterans—not the federal government by way of appropriating money—will be paying for their earned health care. We are outraged." Already, Sisk said, "hundreds of thousands of veterans [are] waiting six months or more for medical appointments."[13] So one wonders whether Vanessa Turner's experience was a "mistake" or a symptom of a bigger problem.

The Bush administration would deny, no doubt, any connection between inadequate funding of the VA system and the "mistakes" that a facility like West Roxbury makes. But people like Turner are giving more than their share from their own meager resources. In fact, in Turner's case, we can see a whole series of parties who help fund this war, mostly invisibly, at their own expense—the USO, the private foundation, Turner herself, and her sister's friend with the crowded apartment. Turner was to find out in mid-2004 whether she's healthy enough to resume active duty. "I'm a soldier," she says. "I love being a soldier."

Although Vanessa Turner paid an especially high price for her contribution to the War on Terror, almost all U.S. military personnel contribute more than their share. One of the most obvious ways is that soldiers buy a lot of their own gear, such as body armor, with their own or their parents' money, because what the U.S. military itself offers them is of low quality.[14]

RESERVES AND NATIONAL GUARD

One the most straightforward economic losses that private citizens absorb in the course of fighting this war falls on members of the armed forces reserves and National Guard. When they are called up for active duty—as more than two hundred thousand were for the war in Iraq—they must leave their jobs, usually taking a large pay cut and often leaving gaps in the companies where they work. A few companies, such as IBM, Target, and J. P. Morgan Chase, make up the difference between military salaries and the civilian pay of their employees and maintain their health insurance. The law does not require them to do so, however, and most companies do not.

Several members of the Minnesota Air National Guard told their stories in mid-2003.[15] Airplane mechanic Robert Mickey's income dropped from $6,000 to $3,000 a month when he was activated for the Iraq war. It was his second call-up in a year; he figures the first cost $12,000. While he was overseas, he was laid off from his civilian job at struggling Northwest Airlines (not because of his absence, but still leaving him with no job to come back to). His wife, Janine, who had been home with their five-year-old, took a full-time job to pay the bills, and the child went into day care at $800 a month.

Scott Sheard was called up two months after 9/11 and was still on active duty a year and a half later. His pay was $1,500 a month less than before, and he lost his base of loyal customers at the Ford dealership where he worked as a salesman. He decided, "With the current world situation, we're likely to be called up again for an unknown period of time," so he gave up on civilian life and decided to join the army full time. Anesthesiologist James Schlimmer was activated as an air force surgeon and had his pay drop by two-thirds. For Brian Schofield, who ran a family dry-cleaning business with his wife, there was no way to make up the income lost. He was activated three days after 9/11 and was still on duty nearly two years later. The Schofields sold the dry-cleaning store and took a 50 percent cut in income. In addition to these kinds of private costs, the public is deprived of the services of the many reservists who are police officers, firefighters, and medical personnel in their civilian roles.

These National Guard members suffered major financial setbacks from the War on Terror. Beyond their personal and emotional sacrifices, they paid a price in money that is all too quantifiable. The government doesn't pay it, and none of it comes from the parking meter in your living room. It comes out of their pockets.

CIVILIANS

Many Americans out of uniform bear disproportional costs from the war as well. I have already mentioned businesses' extra expenses. Volunteers also sacrifice in new ways in wartime. The Seattle volunteer whose story began this book, Vivian Chamberlain, went through a chilly ordeal so that the rest of us would be a little safer in a terrorist attack. And Americans who die and are injured in wars and terrorist attacks represent not only human costs but also economic ones. Each life lost or limited leaves a hole in the economic and social fabric of national life. The person could have worked, earned, invented, and led, thus building wealth and contributing to economic growth. But because of war, that individual will never do so. Based on compensation formulas for 9/11 victims, a single American fatality results in a net loss to the economy on the order of magnitude of $1 million over that person's would-have-been lifetime.

Coming to terms with the real price of war means broadening our view beyond budget items to include other costs that are harder to calculate but no less real. When we look at a veteran suffering flashbacks from post-traumatic stress disorder (PTSD), a factory worker laid off by a company afraid to make investments in uncertain times, or a family struggling to meet rising mortgage payments, we see some of the many faces of the real price of war.

In sum, although war is a net economic loss, not everyone loses or wins equally. Depending how they go, wars can lower oil prices, benefiting big manufacturing companies, or raise them, benefiting oil companies. Thus, Corporate America has conflicting interests regarding war. Some companies do win royally, though. Among individual Americans there are also winners and losers. Notable among those who have given up the most—both personally and economically—are soldiers, especially reservists and National Guard members mobilized for long periods. An important question for political debate is how those costs might be better allocated among the public, so they do not fall so heavily on a few patriotic individuals.

Part Three

FUTURE COSTS AND
HOW WE DIVIDE THEM

Gosh, when it comes to money, I'll take it anywhere I can get it.

—Donald Rumsfeld, March 2002

Chapter Eight

THE PRICE OF FAILURE

The bomb that destroys Chicago would likely arrive not on a missile but in a sport-utility vehicle (SUV). In one minute, one hundred thousand human beings who had been working downtown on an ordinary day either would be dead—the lucky ones—or would have received fatal doses of radiation that would kill them painfully over the coming hours and days. Then again, it could be two hundred thousand people—it's hard to say. Hundreds of thousands more would be permanently injured and sickened. If there were a southeast wind off the lake, the radioactive fallout would severely contaminate the north side—up to O'Hare Airport, Skokie, and Evanston—making the area uninhabitable for years, if not permanently. Millions of Americans would be homeless refugees.

As horrible as this scenario is, the country would survive it. In this sense we have made real progress compared with the Cold War, when the worst-case scenario was the annihilation of the world. But back then, deterrence worked. In this war, deterrence does not work. Even if we knew which corrupt colonel in which country had sold Al Qaeda the nuclear weapon, we could not retaliate in kind. And the cost, in every sense, of a terrorist nuclear attack would defy measurement. Daniel Benjamin and Steven Simon, top counterterrorism officials in the Clinton White House, are not so sure we would survive a single bomb. "Despite the resilience and ingenuity of the American people, a nuclear detonation . . . could be the defeat that precipitates America's decline," they write. Al Qaeda need only be "lucky once with a weapon of mass destruction to trigger an existential crisis for the United States."[1]

Whatever route allowed terrorists to obtain or build a nuclear weapon—a real possibility, as I will show shortly—might very well allow them to get more than one. It would not take many to destroy our economy and way of life. Suppose that the week after Chicago, Dallas blew up, or Miami, or Los Angeles. Not knowing what was coming next, Americans might stream out of the major cities (what would you do?) and bring the economy to a standstill.

How Could It Happen?

The probability of a terrorist nuclear attack may be small but is not negligible. We know, from documents found after Al Qaeda operatives left their bases in Afghanistan, that they were trying to obtain nuclear weapons or the fissionable material to make them and had some weapons design information. In the 1990s, "al-Qaeda's leadership was eager to acquire nuclear arms," as former counterterrorism officials Benjamin and Simon put it, and there is every reason to believe that this interest has only grown stronger with time. Barring a dramatic change, at this moment probably at least one group of Al Qaeda technicians somewhere in the world is drawing up—and perhaps carrying out—plans to try to obtain or build a nuclear weapon. There may be more than one group. While we sleep, they work.

President Bush wrote in September 2002, "Our enemies have openly declared that they are seeking weapons of mass destruction, and evidence indicates that they are doing so with determination."[2] The White House's December 2002 *National Strategy to Combat Weapons of Mass Destruction* (WMD) declares that the "possession and increased likelihood of use of WMD by hostile states and terrorists are realities of the contemporary security environment." Terrorists seek these weapons "with the stated purpose of killing large numbers of our people . . . without compunction and without warning."

According to a 2003 report, Al Qaeda and the Taliban had many "long discussions" with Pakistani nuclear scientists, including a former director of Pakistan's nuclear program who had played "a pioneering role in establishing Pakistan's uranium enrichment project." These were not small fry. And they were personal followers of a Taliban-style Islamic radicalism, who believed that the nuclear bomb rightly belonged to the world Muslim community as a whole. In one meeting in mid-2001, according to the report, "a bin Laden associate indicated that he had nuclear material and wanted to know how to use it to make a weapon." The Pakistani scientists knew how to do that, if indeed the materials at hand were suitable. "It is unknown if they provided enough information to allow Al Qaeda to design a nuclear weapon."[3] The best evidence to date that Al

Qaeda does not have nuclear weapons is that they haven't used one yet.

In 2003, Pakistani nuclear designs—for both uranium enrichment and weapons construction—showed up in Libya and Iran, as they had earlier in North Korea. The Pakistani government claimed the top scientist and several other individuals had acted on their own for financial gain. However, some of the shipments had used government military aircraft, so unanswered questions remained in 2004 about who really controlled Pakistan's nuclear assets. Breaking up the proliferation network was a good thing, made possible when first Iran (hesitantly) and then Libya (wholeheartedly) opened up their secret nuclear programs to international scrutiny. But discovering how extensive the network was came as a shock.

President Bush told Bob Woodward that in late October 2001, "We began to get serious indications that nuclear plans, material and know-how were being moved out of Pakistan." Apparently nothing came of it in the end, but four teams with equipment to detect nuclear materials began "roaming around" Washington, D.C., and New York, a senior official told Woodward.[4]

A month after 9/11, a U.S. intelligence alert from the White House's Counterterrorism Security Group raised the alarm that Al Qaeda might already possess a smallish nuclear weapon from the Russian arsenal and planned to smuggle it into New York City. The alert, based on an intelligence agent of unknown reliability, supposedly coincided with a report from a Russian general who thought he might be missing such a bomb. The government kept its fears secret, even from New York's mayor, to avoid a panic—the account surfaced only five months later. The scare was a false alarm, but the next one might not be. As former senator Sam Nunn, a nonproliferation expert, put it: "This intelligence report, thank God, was later judged to be false. But it was never judged to be implausible or impossible."[5] In November 2001, Osama bin Laden boasted to a Pakistani newspaper that Al Qaeda had chemical and nuclear weapons. He may have meant a radiological weapon, or "dirty bomb"—a conventional bomb laced with radioactive material—which could cause panic but not high casualties. But it was even rumored in the late 1990s that more than twenty nuclear "suitcase bombs" from the former Soviet Union had fallen into bin Laden's hands, via Chechnya. Whatever the U.S. government knows for certain about such rumors and boasts it has not revealed publicly.

Three Routes to the Bomb

There are three basic ways that Al Qaeda or another terrorist group could get nuclear weapons. First, it could obtain—more likely with big bribes than with brazen attacks—one or more working nuclear weapons from the former Soviet arsenal, from Pakistan, or from North Korea. The former Soviet arsenal includes tens of thousands of "tactical" nuclear weapons, made to work with artillery, fighter jets, depth charges, and so forth. Some are lightweight enough to fit in a backpack. With U.S. assistance, Russia has supposedly consolidated all of these, except nobody seems quite sure that the Russians themselves know how many there were and whether all are accounted for. Nor, apparently, are those accounted for entirely secure against theft, especially an inside job. (In addition, there are tens of thousands of "strategic" warheads on long-range vehicles like ballistic missiles; these are more secure.)

Pakistan has far fewer nuclear weapons—"only" some dozens—but Al Qaeda has many supporters in the country. Counterterrorism experts Benjamin and Simon say of Al

Qaeda that "Pakistan is probably their best potential source of the materials, or of the weapons themselves."[6] A Pakistani revolution that replaced the pro-American military dictator with a Taliban-like government—another unlikely but not impossible scenario—would pose a particularly sudden challenge.

North Korea, meanwhile, may already have had one or two working nuclear weapons, and in 2003 it apparently produced half a dozen more.[7] They might go for sale in secret to the highest bidder worldwide, and if one exploded in Chicago, we could probably never prove it came from North Korea. Since 2003, North Korea has been ready, if it so chooses, to open for business as a high-priced candy store for rich terrorists.

Second, a terrorist group could obtain fissionable uranium (a special variety of uranium, hard to make, called U-235). Only national governments command the resources to produce this "enriched" weapons-grade uranium. But there are various quantities floating around, again in the former Soviet Union and other countries. Those other countries may soon include Iran. In early 2003, inspectors led by Mohamed El Baradei of the International Atomic Energy Agency found, in a previously uninspected facility, hundreds of centrifuges ready to begin uranium enrichment, a step that would put Iran in violation of the nuclear nonproliferation treaty it has signed. At the same time, Iran announced its plan to start up a facility to produce the material that goes into those centrifuges. Iran was thus poised to potentially produce enough enriched uranium to start building bombs—or supplying terrorists—within a year or two. In late 2003, Iran agreed to suspend uranium enrichment but will retain its ability to restart nuclear weapons development on short notice.[8]

Worldwide military stocks of highly enriched uranium total about five million pounds, enough to make one hundred thousand nuclear bombs. Another fifty thousand pounds, enough

Box 15 Weapons-grade (highly enriched) uranium worldwide.

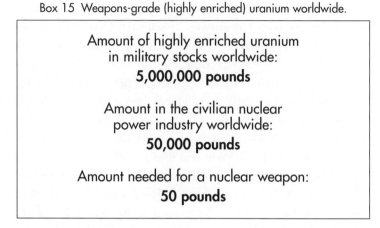

Amount of highly enriched uranium
in military stocks worldwide:
5,000,000 pounds

Amount in the civilian nuclear
power industry worldwide:
50,000 pounds

Amount needed for a nuclear weapon:
50 pounds

for one thousand nuclear bombs, is spread around the civilian nuclear power and nuclear research industry worldwide. Terrorists would need only thirty to one hundred pounds of U-235, depending on the sophistication of the bomb design (see Box 15).[9] The amount of mass actually converted to energy is about that of a penny.

And a uranium bomb is simple to build: Put half the uranium at each end of a tube and shoot one half into the other to create a critical mass and trigger a Hiroshima-size blast. (A critical mass means U-235 dense enough that speeding neutrons from splitting atoms cause other atoms to split in an accelerating chain reaction.) The design of the uranium bomb dropped on Hiroshima in 1945 was never tested—U.S. scientists were certain it would work. (The 1945 Trinity test was of the trickier plutonium design used in the Nagasaki bomb.) Nobel physicist Luis Alvarez calls the design of a uranium nuclear weapon "a trivial job. . . . Even a high school kid could make a bomb in short order." Ted Taylor, a former bomb designer who has sounded the alarm for decades about the inadequate security of nuclear materials, was asked how hard it would be for terrorists to build a nuclear weapon, if given the uranium. His answer: "Very easy. Double underline. Very easy." Thus, highly enriched uranium has been called "the gold standard for terrorists."[10]

Clinton-era counterterrorism officials Benjamin and Simon report that in the 1990s an Al Qaeda operative tried to buy a cylinder reputedly containing uranium of South African origin for a million and a half dollars in Sudan. Benjamin and Simon conclude that it "likely" was not useful material for a weapon or was "one of the many scams" involving sale of supposed nuclear materials. "If the uranium had been weapons grade," they reason, "al Qaeda would have used it by now." While the Sudan cylinder evidently did not live up to its billing, "the desire to procure weapons of mass destruction remained a central ambition of the leaders, some of whom undertook risky travel abroad to see what components they could procure."[11]

A third route for terrorists would be to build a plutonium bomb. Plutonium would be somewhat easier to obtain. The civilian nuclear power industry worldwide has about four hundred thousand pounds, theoretically enough for more than twenty-five thousand bombs at about fifteen pounds per bomb, and the U.S. and Russian military programs have a like amount. However, a plutonium bomb is harder to design than a uranium bomb, since a fissionable core must be pushed in evenly from all sides simultaneously, using high explosives. Pakistan may have used a Chinese design and may have shared designs with North Korea, which in 2003 improved its designs. It is possible that Al Qaeda already has workable designs from the Pakistani nuclear scientists. But on the whole it would strain Al Qaeda's resources actually to manufacture a plutonium bomb rather than steal one. Still, how to do it is no secret. Back in the 1960s, the U.S. government asked two recent physics Ph.D.s with no knowledge of nuclear weapons to design a bomb, using only unclassified information. Their plutonium bomb plan would have worked.[12]

The former Soviet nuclear complex—a prime potential source for terrorists to obtain nuclear materials—urgently needs better security. A 2003 Harvard report finds that in each major category of action, less than half the job is done.[13] "The pace of progress is unacceptably slow," the report concludes. Yet the U.S. program to assist Russia in securing its huge nuclear complex and stockpile of nuclear weapons is underfunded, lacking essential resources. A comprehensive report on nuclear security in November 2003 concluded that "the global community remains alarmingly vulnerable to catastrophic terrorism." Although the Group of Eight (G8) countries had pledged $20 billion the year before to secure nuclear weapons and materials worldwide, only a "tiny fraction" had been spent, the report noted. It identified one hundred poorly protected sites, in forty countries, containing weapons-grade uranium.[14]

President Bush acknowledged in his 2003 State of the Union address that "one crate slipped into this country [could] bring a day of horror like none we have ever known. We will do everything in our power to make sure that that day never comes." But an unnamed U.S. counterterrorism official quoted by *Time* had concluded the year before that "a lot of people are going to die" and "I don't think there's a damn thing we're going to be able to do about it."[15]

What Would It Cost?

The costs of a nuclear attack would be prohibitive. One study on the costs of terrorism in 2002—conducted by the Organization for Economic Cooperation and Development (OECD), a consortium of industrial countries' governments—tried to cost out a twenty-kiloton attack on New York, a task it described as "nearly impossible." (A kiloton equals the power of one thousand tons of conventional explosive.) As a first approximation, it assumed that the city's contribution to the country's GDP would be subtracted, since the attack could "leave most of the metropolitan area uninhabitable for years." That turns out to be about 3 percent of GDP, or about $300 billion per year. In addition, the study notes, the financial industry would be hard hit, transportation would be severely disrupted, business and consumer confidence would be shaken, housing stock outside New York would be overtaxed by surviving New Yorkers, and the federal budget picture would "deteriorate markedly."[16] If you add up these effects, which the study did not, they clearly could add hundreds of billions more to the $300-billion-per-year figure, at least in the first few years.

A Harvard study of a ten-kiloton bomb at New York's Grand Central Station also tried to map out economic effects, combining future costs with immediate ones to get a single total. It concludes that "the sheer economic cost would be staggering." Based on the New York City Comptroller's methodology for calculating economic effects of the 9/11 World Trade Center attack, the Harvard researchers estimated the lost salaries of those killed at close to $1 trillion (about $70,000 per year for twenty-five years on average). The cost of treating the wounded would be at least hundreds of billions of dollars, and the destroyed property and infrastructure well over $100 billion. Lost economic output from the evacuation of Manhattan and the permanent loss of a part of it would add hundreds of billions more. Decontamination of the city could run to another $100 billion. Thus, the direct costs of such an attack would come to at least $1 trillion and possibly several trillion.

Indirect costs, including the possibility that Americans would panic and flee other cities, could multiply these costs.[17]

If, say, three cities were destroyed, the cost would not just triple, but the national disruptions would be much worse and the economic impacts far more severe. The costs could rival our annual GDP of $10 trillion. Even if the GDP began growing again fairly soon, its whole trajectory would be lowered, so that every year for a long time to come the country would be poorer than it would have been. The American standard of living would drop abruptly. The country would survive, and the economy would eventually recover. But the United States would be severely wounded economically and downgraded in terms of world power and stature.

Although this whole calculation is terribly approximate, the order of magnitude is the point. Preventing a single worst-case terrorist attack on U.S. cities would save us much more than *all* war-related spending. So if war spending prevents a nuclear attack, it's worth every penny. I am not talking about *how* the government spends the money. Rather, I am talking about *how much* it spends in this effort. Given the threat, it is not too much. To put it another way, the high cost of winning the war is outweighed by the even higher cost of losing it.

Other Threats

This discussion has focused on a nuclear attack as the worst-case scenario. Other nightmarish possibilities exist, of course. They would be less destructive but could prove highly disruptive to our economy and way of life, perhaps even touching off panic. Probably most likely—because it is relatively easy to pull off, and we know Al Qaeda has been trying—is a "dirty bomb" made from conventional explosives wrapped with radioactive material. This material need not be the hard-to-obtain enriched varieties used in a nuclear weapon, but any kind of medical and industrial radioactive materials available on the international black market. The resulting radiation could contaminate several blocks of a downtown area. The conventional bomb itself would probably kill more people than the radiation would, but property losses and cleanup costs would be high. Residual radioactivity might increase the long-term risks of cancer and other health problems for people in the area. Still, even with the possibility that exaggerated fears could lead millions to flee, dirty bombs pose a much smaller threat than nuclear weapons do.

Chemical weapons, too, would have mainly a psychological effect. Even a successful attack with lethal nerve gas—one that avoided dispersing most of it in the wind—would kill hundreds or thousands, not hundreds of thousands like a nuclear weapon. It would contaminate buildings or city blocks rather than whole cities.

Biological weapons in theory could rival nuclear weapons in lethal power. For example, if Al Qaeda were to obtain genetically modified, vaccine-resistant smallpox virus from a secret program in the former Soviet Union, it could start an epidemic that might kill millions of Americans, in the worst case. But such a worst case is extremely unlikely. (Even if the Soviet Union in fact made such an organism, it is highly improbable that Al Qaeda could get it.) Delivering biological weapons effectively is quite difficult, which is one reason it virtually never has happened in history. And we are getting better prepared to rush in to outbreak sites with quarantines, vaccines, and antibiotics to snuff out an epidemic quickly. Then, too, as Al Qaeda leaders probably understand—their second-in-command is a medical doctor—a biological attack on the United States, Europe, or Israel would likely be contained in those countries but spread out of control through the poor parts of the world, killing far more Muslims than Christians or Jews. Thus, neither biological weapons nor chemical or radiological ones pose a threat comparable to that of nuclear weapons. The term *weapons of mass destruction* is misleading in this regard. We can live with dirty bombs and nerve gas, awful as they would be, but we cannot live with nuclear attacks.

The Home Front Is the Front Line

The frontline troops in this war are not only soldiers in Iraq and Afghanistan but police, firefighters, and others throughout the homeland.

Let's think about how terrorists might get a bomb to Chicago. A disturbingly large number of methods come to mind—a sailboat on Lake Michigan, a drive across the border, a payoff to a port security guard to look the other way. One plausible scenario would be to hide the bomb in the back of a Toyota Land Cruiser SUV, "the official vehicle of jihad" according to former counterterrorism officials Benjamin and Simon.[18] The Land Cruiser's payload of 1,470 pounds is more than enough for a couple of guys out on a camping trip with forged U.S. driver's licenses in the front, and a nuclear bomb in the back with camping and fishing gear. Its range at highway speeds, 432 miles, would get it from, say, Vancouver to Chicago with only four gas stops in Canada and two in the United States. The terrorists would think about such things. With collaborators planted or bought off in a couple of key ports, they might ship the Land Cruiser from South Asia to Fraser River Port, south of Vancouver, tucked into one of the six hundred shipping containers a day passing through the port, most of which are not carefully inspected. Fraser River Port is a major port for imported automobiles, so the arrival of one more new SUV would hardly raise suspicions.

The fishing-trip terrorists could be recruited from new converts of non-Arab background—people like Richard Reid, the British "shoe bomber" of white and Caribbean descent, who nearly blew up a transatlantic flight, or John Walker Lindh, the white American captured in Afghanistan with Taliban fighters. They could drive east across Canada to the border with Minnesota. Funding for Canadian border security was tripled after 9/11, but that's triple a small number for a long, traditionally open border. Once the SUV crosses the sparsely populated and imperfectly patrolled Canada-Minnesota border, it has a straight shot, through Duluth and Wisconsin, to Chicago. But perhaps the terrorists think that we would *expect* them to go straight through Wisconsin to Chicago—that's where we're on the lookout for Jihadmobiles—so they drive due south to Des Moines, Iowa, then straight into Chicago from the west. Twelve hours after crossing the border, the terrorists will destroy central Chicago. Let's follow their route and see how America's homeland defenses look in mid-2003 from the perspective of local communities that are now the front lines of this war.

America's first line of defense south of the border would be the sheriff's deputies of St. Louis County, Minnesota, which stretches from Duluth to the Canadian border. If anyone spotted something suspicious about a Land Cruiser driving south in northern Minnesota, and did anything, it would probably be one of those deputies. Never discount what one alert law enforcement officer can do. When Al Qaeda tried to blow up Los Angeles airport in December 1999, Customs Inspector Diana Dean decided a man driving off a ferry from British Columbia to Washington State "was acting in a nervous and strange manner while answering routine questions." Searching the vehicle, officers found explosives and timing devices hidden in the spare-tire well, thwarting a plot that could have killed hundreds of people.[19] So if you live in Chicago, you want St. Louis County's deputies to be at the top of their game.

But there is a problem. St. Louis County has a shortfall in its $250 million budget. The county raised local property taxes, which pay one-third of the total, by more than 4 percent in 2003. But it still has had to cut spending painfully. The sheriff's department in mid-2003 had eight unfilled positions because of a hiring freeze. It could no longer routinely patrol near the sixty-mile-long Canadian border. When the federal government increased the terror alert status, Sheriff Ross Litman—a ten-year veteran of the force and lifelong resident of the county—did not have the resources to respond adequately. "We're having trouble just doing normal duties rather than dealing with a heightened alert," he told a reporter.[20]

So the SUV drives south, getting on the interstate to Minneapolis. Let's hope the terrorists pass through that city quickly, because Minneapolis is not ready to handle an attack. The police and fire budgets have both been slashed in recent budget cuts. Planned layoffs of police officers were averted at the last minute in June 2003—at the expense of other city services, of course—but no such luck for the firefighters. The fire department had to cut $3.7 million and lay off dozens of firefighters in mid-2003, despite firefighters' vigorous protests to the city council, which had planned even deeper cuts. If terrorists attacked Minneapolis itself, the frontline duties would fall to people like Sean Churchill-Weekes, who trained as an emergency medical technician and firefighter with the Minneapolis Fire Department. In June 2003, Churchill-Weekes heard shots outside his home. He raced outside and helped a critically injured victim of a gang shooting until an ambulance arrived. He didn't fear for his safety, he told a reporter: "You see somebody hurt and you do the job." Trouble is, Churchill-Weekes had just been laid off by the fire department.[21]

The SUV drives on south to Des Moines, Iowa, where the state legislature cut funding to local governments by $60 million in early 2003. Mount Pleasant, Iowa, saved $45,000 by eliminating a police officer position; Dubuque firefighters took their families door to door in mid-2003, asking citizens to oppose the city council's planned cuts.

And it isn't just the Midwest. A recent study by the Federal Emergency Management Agency (FEMA) and the National Fire Protection Association (NFPA) assessed the capabilities and needs of fire departments nationwide in light of their crucial role in homeland security. It found them "underfunded, understaffed, and undertrained" for their new duties, in the words of NFPA president Jim Shannon. "It's not the fault of the fire departments," Shannon said. "They're crying out for the resources." Although the big-city departments are better able to handle a terrorist attack, the smaller departments that would need to come to their aid have serious deficiencies. And even in the biggest and best-prepared departments, nearly 20 percent of personnel involved in hazardous materials response have no formal training for that job. Overall, departments need more portable radios and cannot communicate adequately with federal, state, and local partners in responding to an incident. In 2003 the New York Fire Department needed $276 million to meet priority needs related to homeland security, with more than half of that needed for a new field communication system and a secure backup communications network. New York's training program for handling hazardous materials was understaffed, and a wave of retirements—on top of the firefighters lost on 9/11—left the department younger and less experienced.[22]

Of course, the NFPA represents the interests of the firefighting "industry," so you might suspect their recommendations of higher funding. But the Council on Foreign Relations has no dog in that fight. It set up a Task Force on Emergency Responders to assess the country's readiness to respond to another major terrorist attack. The chairman of the task force was former senator Warren Rudman, one of the nation's leading voices for a balanced budget. His recommendation for emergency response? Spend more money! (Raise taxes and cut other expenditures to pay for it, but do spend it.) The report concluded that we remain "dangerously unprepared to handle" an attack. On *Meet the Press* in June 2003, Rudman sounded the alarm: "We have not taken care of emergency responders. . . . They just don't have the funding, the training, the personnel that if tomorrow, a major WMD—weapons of mass destruction—attack were to take place in a major American city, we are not prepared to deal with it, and those are flat-out facts." When asked if the problem "always comes down . . . to money," Rudman replied, "Absolutely." Solving the problem, he said, would take about $100 billion over five years, which would be a tripling of expenditures. The Department of Homeland Security responded, defensively, that the Council on Foreign Relations report "grossly inflated" the funding needs and wanted "to install gold-plated telephones." Rudman replied, "We don't want gold-plated telephones. We would like radios that work, and we don't have them."[23]

Another 2003 report surveyed police and firefighters in forty U.S. cities and towns. A majority, it found, "feel vastly underprepared and underprotected for the consequences of chemical, biological, or radiological attacks." The available hazardous materials gear, it found, was intended for industrial accidents and "is neither designed nor certified for this new role of terrorism response."[24]

Driving on to Chicago, the terrorists would enter a city with a secret disaster response plan thicker than a phone book. Chicago has increased the fire department budget in recent years, and after four years without a contract or cost-of-living raise, the firefighters' union finally got a contract agreement in 2003, with back pay. The department is even getting 120 thermal imaging cameras, to "see" through smoke, courtesy of a banking executive's personal million-dollar donation (after he lost friends in the World Trade Center attack).[25] Like other big-city terrorist targets, Chicago has put considerable effort into trying to prepare for a terrorist attack. Unfortunately, if there *were* a nuclear bomb in the back of the Toyota Land Cruiser, Chicago's extensive disaster resources would be a day late and a dollar short.

What Might Happen?

The effects of a nuclear weapon depend on its explosive power. The uranium bomb that the United States dropped on Hiroshima in 1945 and the plutonium bomb dropped on Nagasaki three days later had explosive power of fifteen to twenty kilotons. This size bomb is most likely for a terrorist attack. A crude design or botched job might produce a bomb with only a tenth of this power, whereas a stolen weapon from the former Soviet arsenal might be ten times as destructive. (By standards of today's nuclear arsenals, Hiroshima was a low-yield weapon.) But the most probable scenario is a Hiroshima-sized bomb.

The Hiroshima bomb killed about one hundred thousand people. Many of them died instantly, but many died painfully from radiation over days and weeks, and survivors suffered lifelong health problems from radiation exposure, notably cancers. A similar attack on a U.S. city today would produce at least that level of casualties, probably several times more. A 2002 report estimated that a smaller ten-kiloton bomb detonated in lower Manhattan would kill one hundred thousand and sicken seven hundred thousand with radiation. A circle of property and people half a mile in diameter would be completely destroyed, and the spillover would cripple the entire city and overwhelm the nation.[26]

The Harvard report on nuclear weapons and materials, mentioned earlier, estimated the effects of a ten-kiloton bomb set off at Grand Central station in Manhattan on an average workday (a more deadly location than assumed in the 2002 study). "More than half a million people would likely be killed by the immediate effects of the explosion, from the combination of blast, heat, radiation, and building collapse." Hundreds of thousands would be severely injured, and "every bed in every hospital for a hundred miles would not be remotely sufficient to handle the casualties." Downwind, depending on weather conditions, tens to hundreds of thousands more would receive enough radiation to kill them slowly. If the wind were blowing north, all of Manhattan would likely become uninhabitable, turning millions of New Yorkers into refugees.[27] Thus, although the world wars in their global scope were much larger than the War on Terror—even if it claims Chicago and Dallas—nonetheless, in terms of *American* casualties and economic costs, the scale could be comparable (see Box 16).

President Bush was briefed on the danger of a terrorist nuclear attack by CIA director George Tenet in late October 2001, in the White House Situation Room. According to the *Washington Post*, the briefing "sent the President through the roof," and he instructed the government to make the problem its top priority. Making permanent an emergency evacuation that started on September 11, all the major U.S. government

Box 16 Comparing war fatalities.

Number of Americans killed in World War II:
400,000

Number of Americans who might be killed
by a single terrorist nuclear weapon:
100,000–500,000?

agencies began sending high-level managers to live for months on end, around the clock, in secure underground control centers outside Washington, D.C., left over from the Cold War. The officials in these bunkers, about one hundred people, cannot tell even their families where they are going or why. They form a government-in-waiting that would run the country if a nuclear attack destroyed Washington, D.C. They would try to maintain the country's vital systems—food and water supply, transportation, energy, communications, and public health. Right now they are still down there in the bunkers, waiting. Without them, one official told the *Washington Post*, a nuclear attack on Washington "would be 'game over.'"[28]

To conclude, if we do not pay the bill to defeat terrorism, our cities could be destroyed. This chapter has shown how real such a threat is, and how inadequate our responses to this threat have been. The country is not ready.

Chapter Nine

A WAR WITHOUT SACRIFICE?

If you have a rug in your living room, it makes a great place to sweep the dust under if company is at the door and you're not finished cleaning. But suppose you tried to hide an elephant under there? That strategy pretty well sums up what President Bush has tried to do with the costs of the War on Terror. According to him, nobody should pay more taxes because of this war. Indeed, everyone should pay less, especially the rich. Middle-class voters should not have to give up their American way of life, lower their expectations, pay more for consumer goods or for mortgages, trade in their gas-guzzling SUVs, forgo new prescription drug benefits, or in any other way pay a price to accomplish the difficult work of the War on Terror.

The president set the tone of a war without sacrifice in his speech to Congress nine days after 9/11. It was a defining speech, rallying the country and setting its new direction. The War on Terror, he warned, would be "a lengthy campaign," drawing on "every resource at our command." America would remain united and resolute: "We will not tire, we will not falter, and we will not fail." The speech was well received, but one point was missing: Whose money and energies would pay for this effort? Bush did not ask us to shoulder the costs of the new, open-ended war. Rather, he said, "Americans are asking: What is expected of us? I ask you to live your lives, and hug your children"—as well as cooperate with law enforcement, be patient with inconveniences, pray, and continue to show "confidence in the American economy."[1] Translation: Go shopping! That'll show the terrorists and dictators. Congress followed suit by dramatically increasing military spending while cutting taxes, bringing back deep deficits in the federal budget.

Bush's speech did not discuss the threat posed by Al Qaeda's possible use of weapons of mass destruction against American cities. Bob Woodward, in *Bush at War*, quotes the president as telling his inner circle on the morning of the speech that he had removed that section: "I took it out. It's going to stay out. I thought long and hard about it. . . . Need to be honest, but I don't know about being brutally honest." Describing threats to Bush's own safety a few weeks after 9/11, Woodward writes that the president and his wife "had several ways of dealing with threats, and one was denial." Laura Bush described it to Woodward as "a sort of fatalism," and the president added, "If it's meant to be, it's going to happen. And therefore there's no need to try to hide from a terrorist."[2]

We are all in denial about this war—a continuing war against both known and unknown threats to our nation. Because war is traumatic and horrible, we try to compartmentalize it in our minds, our lives, and our society. We resist coming to terms with the high costs of fighting a long war of global scope and terrifying potential. Denial is a very comfortable stance because it allows one to continue with business, or politics, as usual. But denial is no basis for national policy. We can be fatalistic about our own lives—even the president can—but not about losing Chicago.

Cutting Corners

President Bush promised to do "everything in our power" to keep weapons of mass destruction from harming American cities. But his money was not where his mouth was. Funds for the war increased, but not enough to win, because of competing demands on the federal budget and the country's political attention. Specifically, Bush's economic priority was massive tax cuts for wealthy Americans, which he considered the best medicine for a sluggish economy.

Democrats for their part also shortchanged the war effort, favoring stimulation of the economy by such means as universal health insurance, targeted tax cuts, extended unemployment benefits, and social safety-net programs. (They did favor more money for homeland security, but that's easy politically since it creates jobs for constituents.) Several Democratic presidential candidates in 2004 wanted to reverse Bush's tax cuts, but not in order to put the money into war spending and keep tightening our belts on domestic programs. This bipartisan effort left the War on Terror with neither the economic resources nor the nation's undivided attention needed to win. The failure to mobilize the country has held back the war effort. Consider three examples.

First, in the war in Afghanistan in late 2001, we succeeded in ousting the Taliban from power at a modest cost (on the order of magnitude of $10 billion) and with very low U.S. casualties.

But if we had spent more and been more willing to take casualties, we might well have captured or killed Osama bin Laden and other top Al Qaeda leaders. Reportedly, bin Laden was hiding in the caves of Tora Bora in eastern Afghanistan as we were bombing them. But U.S. commanders did not want to send in U.S. ground forces to surround and destroy those Al Qaeda forces—U.S. casualties are politically unpopular—and the fighters slipped away, with bin Laden, over the mountains into the tribal areas of western Pakistan. They regrouped and continued to attack U.S. targets worldwide, even gaining strength as rising anti-Americanism fueled extremism.

Journalist Daniel Bergner in July 2003 described the continuing war by eighty-five hundred U.S. troops in Afghanistan. "Ninety percent of bin Laden's forces"—some eighteen thousand graduates of Al Qaeda training camps in Afghanistan—"and over half of his top commanders, remain free. And no one is quite sure where they are." U.S. forces last had a fix on bin Laden among a thousand fighters heading to the Pakistan border around Thanksgiving 2001, Bergner reported. But, Bergner wrote, "the American high command . . . didn't want to put its soldiers—even Delta Force, renowned for risk-taking—in severe danger; didn't want British special forces—who also had teams in the area, eager to move in—to claim the war's greatest prize; and couldn't compel Pakistan to close off the frontier." According to Bob Woodward, the CIA official responsible for the operation concluded that "the Afghan tribals . . . had done a sorry job. Also, there had been poor coordination with the Pakistanis and there had been no Plan B." This official "believed that . . . bin Laden walked or rode by mule into Pakistan with a core group of about a dozen outriders." A *Newsweek* report in August 2002 gave a blow-by-blow account of Al Qaeda's escape, including the support its fighters received from sympathetic villagers and local guides along the way.[3] Thus, bin Laden got at least two years of extra time to see his organization through a transition so that it could carry on without the sanctuary of Afghanistan. In 2003, Al Qaeda and related groups continued terror attacks worldwide—in Morocco, Saudi Arabia, Russia, the Philippines, Indonesia, Iraq, and Turkey.

After the liberation of the capital, Kabul, the United States did not extend security to the rest of Afghanistan. Journalist Nicholas Kristof, who saw firsthand the bandit-ridden Afghan countryside, described the U.S. hesitation to extend security there as creating "petri dishes for terrorists." In February 2002 he argued that "helping war-torn third-world countries is a smarter policy than running away from them." Yet, Kristof complained, "President Bush continues to stiff Afghanistan's caped hero, Hamid Karzai, as he pleads for American troops to help secure all of Afghanistan." As Kristof wrote a few months later, "Is there any explanation other than inertia to account for the United States' maintaining 47,000 troops in Japan, despite the lack of any threat there except perhaps from extraterrestrials, yet refusing to provide a few thousand troops to keep the swamp drained in Afghanistan?"[4]

So what complaint did Defense Secretary Rumsfeld return to six times at a March 2002 briefing about the issue of countrywide security in Afghanistan? Money. Not enough of it. Deploying peacekeepers across the country would be expensive, and other countries "are not offering troops; nor are they offering money," Rumsfeld complained. Building up an Afghan national army would also be expensive. But a recent donors conference—nations pledging aid for Afghanistan—had come up with "not a nickel" for either peacekeepers or an Afghan national army. Until there was money to do one or both of these tasks, security could not be extended to the country from the capital, Rumsfeld said. And then this: "I wish there were money for it. And we're going to try to raise some. And I think we now have an amount, if I'm not mistaken, don't we?" Rumsfeld turned to the nation's top military commander, General Richard Myers, who replied gamely: "I think we have a little bit, sir." When asked which countries should contribute, Rumsfeld replied, "Gosh, when it comes to money, I'll take it anywhere I can get it."[5]

A year and half after that briefing, most of Afghanistan remained under warlord control, with the influence of the pro-American government largely limited to the capital city where a fifty-five-hundred member UN-approved NATO peacekeeping force kept order. The Bush administration, focused on Iraq, had not galvanized the money or support to extend the peacekeeping force to the rest of the country. NATO began planning tentative moves beyond the capital in late 2003, but in January 2004 a top NATO general, James L. Jones, told a Senate committee that allies were not providing enough troops for Afghanistan. Civilian aid agencies and the United Nations meanwhile complained that the lack of security outside the capital was a major impediment to humanitarian assistance. The top U.S. general in Afghanistan in 2002–3, after returning to Fort Bragg, North Carolina, said that aid projects like roads were lagging, and that Pakistani forces in the border provinces were not effectively preventing incursions of Al Qaeda and Taliban, whose forces seriously threatened the Afghan government. The Afghan national army was just picking up momentum after a slow start. Many recruits to that army in 2002 soon quit because the U.S.-paid salary of $30 a month was too low (see Box 17).[6] The president promised to put "every resource at our command" into the War on Terror, but then paid these guys a dollar a day to fight our enemies.

Finally, in late summer 2003, the administration concluded that it needed to increase spending in Afghanistan, including nearly doubling reconstruction aid, which was below $1 billion

Box 17 Going cheap in Afghanistan.

U.S.-paid salary of a soldier in the
new Afghan national army, 2002:
$1 per day

Income the UN defines as "extreme poverty"
in poor countries:
$1 per day or less

a year. Too bad about waiting a year and a half to start, though. And how long will it take to realize that even $2 billion a year isn't enough to accomplish the mission?

Our reticence to spend on Afghanistan was not due to U.S. public opinion: A poll in July 2003, even as Americans were dying daily in Iraq, found that U.S. voters by more than two to one supported extending the UN force to the whole of Afghanistan and contributing U.S. troops to it, provided other countries also contributed. Although the public showed widespread confusion about who does control the Iraqi countryside and where UN forces are, pollster Steven Kull pointed out the public's "belief that instability and lawlessness can make Afghanistan continue to be a breeding ground for terrorist organizations."[7]

President Bush's unwillingness to commit more resources and accept more costs in the Afghan war—by using U.S. forces instead of Afghan warlords to pursue bin Laden, and by paying for peacekeepers or an Afghan national army to provide countrywide security—was penny-wise and pound-foolish.

A second example is the war in Iraq. After a smashing victory in taking over the country, U.S. forces were stretched too thin, and wrongly equipped, to maintain public order. Looting, rape, and murder went unchecked week after week, triggering Iraqi anger against the Americans. The country's infrastructure—electricity, water, oil—which had been largely spared by American smart bombs, was gutted by looters, setting reconstruction way back. Before long, more Iraqis were shooting at the Americans, and U.S. forces found Iraqis' hearts and minds turning against them. By August 2003, with U.S. troops dying in Iraq, Thomas Friedman argued that to win in Iraq—"the Big One" for American interests in the whole Middle East and thus the War on Terror—"we need an American public, and allies, ready to pay any price and bear any burden, but we have a president unable or unwilling to summon either." We didn't pay the new Iraqi Army soldiers $1 a day, as we did in Afghanistan. We paid $2 a day—not enough to live on in Iraq. Only after a wave of desertions did the U.S. commander in Iraq agree in December 2003 to review the pay issue.[8]

At the same time, the U.S. government also tried to go cheap in supplying and supporting our troops in Iraq. Editorials in the pro-military newspaper *Army Times* blasted President Bush and the Republican-controlled Congress for breaking promises of support and benefits for the military. "Talk is cheap," the paper complained in July 2003, "and getting cheaper by the day, judging from the nickel-and-dime treatment the troops are getting lately." The editorial criticizes the administration for opposing an increase—from $6,000 to $12,000—in the payment made to families of troops killed on active duty, and for proposing reductions in imminent-danger pay ($250 down to $150 a month) and family-separation allowance ($250 down to $100 a month). Tax relief measures for military personnel and veterans were stalled, and the budget request for 2004 would cut more than $1 billion from military construction, leaving a "bleak" outlook for "crumbling military housing and other facilities," according to the paper.[9]

The government also underspent on a program to buy up the shoulder-fired antiaircraft missiles in Saddam's arsenal. These missiles pose an acute threat to commercial aviation, which is vital to the global economy. Al Qaeda had already tried to used them in Kenya (narrowly missing a passenger jet), and many had been fired at U.S. aircraft in Iraq. The missiles fetched $5,000 apiece on a thriving international black market, and Iraq in 2003 overflowed with criminal thugs and religious extremists who provided the means and motive, respectively, to sell these missiles to terrorists. To take away their opportunity, U.S. military forces in Iraq bought up several hundred of them, offering a reward for anyone turning one in—total cost, just over $100,000.[10] That's a real bargain to remove a prime opportunity for terrorists to disrupt the global economy. In fact, it was too much of a bargain. Since we paid only $500 apiece for the missiles, Iraqis of shady character could get two or three times our price and middlemen could still make a big profit reselling on the black market. Only a fraction of the missile arsenal was recovered. Because of the threat from these missiles, the Baghdad airport remained closed to commercial traffic a year after the fall of Saddam's regime, impeding reconstruction and humanitarian assistance and raising the ultimate cost to U.S. taxpayers.

Had President Bush sent in more troops—especially military police, soldiers trained as peacekeepers, and Arabic speakers—we could have gotten off to a good start instead of a bad one in Iraqi reconstruction, gaining Iraqis' trust and protecting infrastructure from looting. Again, penny-wise and pound-foolish.

Third, "first responders" are the front line of the War on Terror at home, as Chapter 8 showed. Police and fire departments, along with hospitals and local agencies, are the ones who must move into the action when others are fleeing it. As we remember from 9/11, they go up the stairs when everyone else is going down.[11] Fire departments need new equipment and training for their new duties in the War on Terror. But they don't have enough money. In the local and state budget crises, and lacking adequate federal assistance, police and fire departments have lost funding like most other agencies. In the supplemental funding bill after 9/11, the Republican Congress *cut out* most of the money—several billion dollars—that was to pay for first responders in local communities. (Closer to the 2004 election, Congress did approve such funding.)

In mid-2003, the American Red Cross, which would play a crucial role in responding to any attack, had to cut its spending by millions of dollars and lay off hundreds of its workers. The group's Web site in mid-2003 announced that the Red Cross was desperately short of money, with its disaster relief fund at the lowest point in eleven years, and that the nation's blood banks urgently needed more blood donors because of "critically low" supplies of blood. The funding shortages and cutbacks affecting first providers could mean the difference between success and failure at containing an epidemic sparked by a biological weapon, such as smallpox or plague. By spending more money, we could increase our chances of saving many lives.

These examples show that although we spend a lot on this war, and give it a lot of attention, it will likely require even more money and attention in the next four years. There is no cheap solution to our number-one problem.

Burnout

One sign of trying to accomplish huge tasks with inadequate resources is burnout among the key personnel responsible for the effort. A disturbing pattern of the Bush administration's first two years at war is the high turnover of counterterrorism officials whose experience is needed to fight this peculiar kind of war successfully.

Rand Beers quit, before the war in Iraq, as special assistant to President Bush and senior director for combating terrorism. He then became an adviser to a Democratic presidential candidate, Senator John Kerry of Massachusetts, to whom Beers was attracted as a fellow Vietnam veteran. A Brookings Institution scholar, Paul C. Light, said, "I can't think of a single example in the last 30 years of a person who has done something so extreme" in the Washington bureaucracy.[12] Whether or not you agree with Beers's conclusion about Bush, he is one of the few people who saw the War on Terror from the inside before, during, and after the rise of Al Qaeda and the 9/11 attacks, so his complaints deserve a listen.

This is Rand (Randy) Beers: age sixty; married; two children; resident of Washington, D.C.; born in Washington, D.C.; college degree from Dartmouth; U.S. Marines, 1964–68, Vietnam; master's degree, Michigan, 1971; government service 1971–2003, including multiple positions in the State Department (narcotics, counterterrorism, policy planning), National Security Council (NSC) staff in four administrations (Reagan, Bush I, Clinton, and Bush II), and senior adviser to Supreme Allied Commander, Europe; special assistant to the president, 2002. A colleague from the NSC of the first Bush administration called him "your model government worker. He works for the common good of the American people. He's fair, balanced, honest." Beer resigned from government in March 2003—for "personal reasons," the White House said.[13]

This is what Beers told the *Washington Post* a few months after he resigned: "The administration wasn't matching its deeds to its words in the war on terrorism. They're making us less secure, not more secure. . . . The difficult, long-term issues both at home and abroad have been avoided, neglected or shortchanged and generally underfunded." Homeland security, he said, suffers from "policy constipation. Nothing gets done." It's all talk—"a rhetorical policy." The Department of Homeland Security is underfunded, and "we are asking our firemen, policemen, Customs and Coast Guard to do far more with far less than we ever ask of our military." The Afghanistan operation? "Terrorists move around the country with ease. We don't even know what's going on. Osama bin Laden could be almost anywhere in Afghanistan." The Iraq operation? An "ill-conceived and poorly executed strategy." The only bright spot for Beers is the CIA, doing more jobs competently. Beers concluded that the administration was "underestimating the enemy."[14]

Later, on *Nightline*, Beers added, "Firstly, there is an inadequate amount of funding" for homeland security, with port security and the chemical industry standing out as vulnerable points. The administration, he said, had "been unable or unwilling to ask for sufficient funds to actually do the job." Overseas, "the manpower and the money that I thought were necessary for Afghanistan were simply not there." When asked if he resigned out of exhaustion or frustration with policy, Beers said, "I resigned because I was deeply concerned about the policy and did not see that policy changing. And because I was exhausted trying to make the policy work."[15]

You might think that Beers had borne his share of the burden in protecting his country after his time in Vietnam, or after his three decades of government service under both parties. But he paid an especially high price in his last job. Every day, five hundred to one thousand pieces of information about terrorist threats crossed his desk. (Nobody wanted to filter out information in case something happened and they would be to blame.) Beers's job was to make sense of it all and to try to mobilize the administration to respond. "It's a monstrous responsibility," a colleague of Beers on Clinton's NSC staff, William Wechsler, said. "You sit around every day, thinking about how people want to kill thousands of Americans." Beers himself said, "The first day, I came in fresh and eager. On the last day, I came home tired and burned out. And it only took seven months."[16]

Bush administration supporters have criticized Beers for whining. Columnist Robert Novak wrote that the "resignation of a senior national security aide on policy grounds followed by defection to the political opposition is unprecedented" and called Beers a "defector"—harsh language in wartime. Rather than conclude that counterterrorism efforts may need more attention and maybe even more money, Novak draws this conclusion from the episode: Letting Beers, "a registered Democrat," hold a "highly sensitive post in a Republican administration was an accident bound to happen."[17]

Again, this book is not about *how* we fight the War on Terror, so Beers's departure would not be relevant if he just disagreed with policy and quit. That's what three U.S. diplomats did to protest the administration's Iraq policy, and what five others did a decade before to protest President Clinton's Bosnia policy. Similarly, in August 2003, on the eve of talks with North Korea, Jack Pritchard, the leading expert on North Korea in the State Department—one of the few people having hands-on experience with that unpredictable regime—resigned, then publicly criticized the administration's Korea policies. (He favored using both carrots and sticks, his superiors only sticks.) These disagreements happen in all administrations. The reason Beers's resignation and "defection" to the Democrats matter here is his reason for quitting—not because our policies to fight terrorism were wrong but simply that they were not getting the money and attention they needed.

When Beers quit his job, he drove over to Dick Clarke's house to share a bottle of wine and talk. They had much in common. Clarke served in the State Department in the Reagan and Bush I administrations and headed counterterrorism efforts in the Clinton White House. To hear Clinton-era NSC officials Benjamin and Simon tell it, Dick Clarke was the unstoppable force that single-handedly got the government bureaucracy to take seriously the terrorism threat and change business-as-usual in the late 1990s. He got the Pentagon to put missiles on the unmanned Predator drone in three months instead of the planned three years. He was kept on by the Bush administration but given less attention and power than before. Former chairman of the Joint Chiefs of Staff Hugh Shelton told Benjamin and Simon that Clarke "wasn't at the top of their priority list."[18] After 9/11, Clarke was reassigned to cybersecurity issues. In January 2003, reportedly faced with a further downgrading of his position as it moved into the new Department of Homeland Security, Clarke resigned. So he was home with the bottle of wine when Randy Beers drove up.

When Clarke was shifted to cybersecurity in late 2001, his replacement was retired army general Wayne A. Downing. But General Downing also quit abruptly, in mid-2002. It wasn't over Iraq policy—he was gung-ho to overthrow Saddam and, if anything, frustrated with how long the Pentagon wanted to take about it. Rather, a Republican defense expert told the *Washington Post*, Downing "thought he would have involvement in all sorts of things that it turned out he isn't involved in. And he wasn't allowed to do the things he thought he was hired to do." Former counterterrorism official Larry C. Johnson said that Downing "was unhappy with the bureaucracy." An unnamed security expert told the *Post* that "homeland security is a fiasco, and that's probably why" Downing quit.[19]

Over at the FBI, the head of counterterrorism, Larry Mefford, resigned in October 2003—the third person to quit that job in fourteen months. Each of the three had led the effort to reinvent the FBI with a mission of preventing terrorist attacks, rather than its historical mission of solving and prosecuting past crimes. Reportedly, the job with its fourteen-hour days was as exhausting as Rand Beers's at the NSC.[20]

Evidently, the government's top officials charged with winning the War on Terror are not getting what they need to succeed. Instead, the Bush administration treats the people in these jobs like light bulbs: Burn them until they burn out, then screw a new one in. In my view, they are more like canaries in the mine, telling us as they drop one by one that the War on Terror is not getting what it needs, that we are not winning. Many Americans and most of our friends around the world don't even think we're moving forward.

In conclusion, Americans are in denial about the substantial war costs we face. The Bush administration has not asked the American people to sacrifice for the war effort. But the costs will not disappear. However we fight the war, and whatever combination of military and nonmilitary means we use to win it, the war effort itself depends on the ability of the country to muster the needed resources and political will. In the end, most Americans *will* have to sacrifice to pay the costs of war in the coming years. We can borrow money now and try to push the costs off onto the next generation. We can let creeping inflation nibble at our pocketbooks to make up the difference. We can cut social programs—damaging health care, public education, and our crumbling infrastructure—and thus multiply the social costs of poverty in the long run. We can raise taxes. But the costs will not just disappear. The idea of a war without sacrifice is a lie.

Chapter Ten

SHARING THE BURDEN

Coming out of denial and coming to terms with the costs of war will mean closing a gap in the Bush administration between words and deeds—between George W. Bush's promise to do "everything in our power" to win the War on Terror and Donald Rumsfeld's "Gosh, when it comes to money, I'll take it anywhere I can get it." Congressional Democrats were quick to criticize what they called a "credibility gap" in Bush's homeland security speech in February 2003. They contrasted rhetoric such as "Inspectors will be posted at more than 20 ports around the world" with actions such as failing to request funding for the initiative. The Democrats said that port security overall cost about $1 billion in the first year, but the administration budget included no money for port security grants, and congressional Republicans came up with only $250 million on their own. In early 2002, the administration turned down the immigration authorities' request for $50 million to hire hundreds of agents to track down foreigners who overstay their visas.[1]

The big issue is what happens beyond the 2004 election. Expect 2005 to be the year of bearing the burden of war. Right after a presidential election, and not right before the next one, is the best time to impose costs, inflict pain, and make enemies. The president, whether Bush or Kerry, will have a big unfinished agenda around the world. Meanwhile, easy sources of money and one-time accounting tricks will be used up, spiraling deficits may be getting dicey, and state budgets may still be strained. Fasten your seat belt.

Politics, Interest Groups, and War Needs

So the real question is not how much we pay—a lot, and probably more in the coming years—but how we pay it. Unfortunately for purposes of paying for war, the needs of the war often conflict with other political goals across a range of issue areas. Competition for budget dollars is one major aspect, but it goes beyond that. The best interests of the war effort often compete against the interests of various domestic U.S. constituencies.

A creed of self-interest dominates politics today. Democracy now seemingly consists of an array of divergent interest groups paying their admission at the door—to campaign committees—and then competing to divide up the pie. Just as the invisible hand is supposed to make economic marketplaces efficient, so the pulling and tugging of self-interested parties is supposed to produce policies that are in the society's overall interest. We elevate greed to a virtue.

But there is a problem. Our individual self-interest lies in shirking duty, neglecting the group, and taking advantage of others. From corporate polluters to Iraqi looters, societies always contain individuals who will enrich themselves at the expense of others, unless there is a strong government to enforce laws. Similarly, large enterprises such as war could not be accomplished without a government to collect taxes and allocate money for the task.

To overcome individual self-interest and get people to sacrifice for a common goal requires leadership. Here's how John F. Kennedy tried to summon the collective effort to wage the Cold War, during his inaugural address in 1961: "Since this country was founded," he told America's assembled political leaders, "each generation of Americans has been summoned to give testimony to its national loyalty. The graves of young Americans who answered the call to service surround the globe. Now the trumpet summons us again." He promised that "we shall pay any price, bear any burden, meet any hardship, support any friend, oppose any foe to assure the survival and the success of liberty." And he closed the deal with the sentence we remember him best for: "And so, my fellow Americans: ask not what your country can do for you—ask what you can do for your country."

Similarly, Kennedy tried to rouse the international community to overcome individual interests for a common purpose: "To those old allies whose cultural and spiritual origins we share, we pledge the loyalty of faithful friends. United there is little we cannot do. . . . Divided there is little we can do—for we dare not meet a powerful challenge at odds and split asunder. . . . To that world assembly of sovereign states, the United Nations, our last best hope in an age where the instruments of war have far outpaced the instruments of peace, we renew our pledge of support."[2] This kind of political leadership that elicits sacrifices—of the individual citizen for the nation and of individual nations for shared international goals like defeating terrorism—is what was missing in the early years of the War on Terror. Instead, politics has been all about what your country can do for you.

Tax Cuts

Two key Republican goals—cutting taxes and winning the war—directly conflict. In 2003, as Iraq costs mounted, many commentators made the connection. Columnist Ronald Brownstein put it this way: "Old question: What did you do in the war, Daddy? New answer: I pocketed a large tax cut, honey. (Pause.) And then I passed the bill for the war onto you."[3]

The costs of the war in Iraq did convince the Senate to cut in half President Bush's proposed 2003 round of tax cuts—a proposal Bush had brought to Congress at the height of his popularity after he declared victory in Iraq. Instead of Bush's requested $700 billion plus over ten years, Congress approved $330 billion over ten years. Three Republicans sided with the Democratic senators to reduce the package, including George Voinovich of Ohio, who said, "I think the war has given everyone a more sober look at things." Democratic Senator Russell Feingold of Wisconsin explained the Democrats' success thus: "People were starting to get sensitive about the budget not being honest about the war. And Republicans were under a lot of pressure to acknowledge that the tax cut runs at cross-purposes with fighting this war."[4]

The 2003 round of tax cuts, coinciding with the liberation of Iraq, did not pass on a wave of public support. On the contrary: In April 2003, as Congress debated the cuts, an Associated Press poll found Americans by two to one in favor of holding off on

Box 18 House Republicans' priorities.

"Nothing is more important in the face of a war
than cutting taxes."
                    —Tom DeLay, Republican leader in the
                          House of Representatives, 2003

additional tax cuts to ensure there was adequate money for the
war effort. Congress passed $330 billion in new tax cuts any-
way (see Box 18).[5]

An Honest Accounting

Here's a different story. In his State of the Union address, the
president told Congress that the world had become a more dangerous place in the preceding year. He urged a plan for "mobi-
lization and defense" that would "involve of course very large
additional expenditures of money, expenditures which will con-
siderably exceed the estimated revenues of the government."
Not content with vague concepts, the president put a price tag
on the additional defense expenses he was requesting: $1.6 bil-
lion, measured in today's dollars. He projected the deficit, $5
billion, but noted it could be reduced to $2 billion by keeping
present taxes in place rather than reducing them as Congress
had planned. The deficit *could* be closed by borrowing money,
the president noted, but "I, for one, do not believe that the people of this country approve of postponing the payment of their
bills. Borrowing money is short-sighted finance." Rather, "we
should pay as we go." And from what source? Most or all
should come from modestly increasing income taxes on those

who can afford it. Smaller amounts should come from excise taxes on gasoline, automobiles, iron, and steel.

It's pretty obvious that this pay-as-you-go president was not George W. Bush. It was, in fact, Woodrow Wilson, in December 1915. World War I was raging in Europe, and the United States, though still neutral, needed battleships badly. Wilson thought the American people, and the Congress, would step forward gladly to pay the bills. "Borrowing money," he said, "can be justified only when permanent things are to be accomplished which many generations will certainly benefit by and which seems hardly fair that a single generation should pay for." He had in mind the bond-financed building of the Panama Canal—still in use a century later. Building up U.S. defenses before the country's entry into World War I did not qualify, in Wilson's view, "except in the sense that everything wisely done may be said to be done in the interest of posterity as well as in our own." But that wasn't enough to justify debt. (When the United States itself entered World War I in 1917, it needed both debt *and* higher taxes to pay the bills.) President Wilson was as straightforward about war expenses as he could be. He felt that "the people of the country are entitled to know just what burdens of taxation they are to carry." The president did not gloss over costs and run up debts, even though he was up for reelection in less than a year. (He won.)[6]

Sure, George W. Bush is not Woodrow Wilson; but that's beside the point. The point is that in 1915 you could have an honest political dialogue among the president, the Congress, and the American people about the real costs of running a government in wartime—how much is needed and where it should come from. In today's political climate, politicians would risk their own defeat—beginning with a drop in political campaign contributions from monied interests—by calling for higher income taxes to pay war costs, as Woodrow Wilson did in 1915.

Today's political discourse takes for granted magic money that lets the president and Congress do everything—war, tax cuts, and Medicare prescription drug benefits—without pesky financial constraints.

Interest Group versus National Interest

Each industry and state and economic class has interests in how the costs of war are paid—preferably by someone else. If the system fails to produce national consensus on who should contribute what, the war effort may lack the resources it needs.

Take Pakistan. The U.S. national interest is to keep Pakistan's government as an ally, win over Pakistani public opinion, and support Pakistan's actions against terrorists near the Afghan border. Let's see how these national interests conflict with the interests of U.S. taxpayers and interest groups.

Pakistan's military ruler, President Pervez Musharraf, has been a staunch U.S. ally in the War on Terror, despite tremendous anti-Americanism in his society. (A poll early in 2004 found that 65 percent of Pakistanis held a favorable view of bin Laden and an unfavorable view of President Bush.) Reportedly, Musharraf arrested and turned over to U.S. custody hundreds of terrorist suspects captured in Pakistan. During the war in Afghanistan in late 2001, among U.S. policy makers "everyone understood that President Musharraf was the crucial barrier between stability and a worst-case scenario," writes Bob Woodward.[7] Musharraf allowed U.S. planes to use Pakistani bases and went out on a limb domestically to give the U.S. government what it demanded. In elections in 2002, radical Islamists won control of the two western provincial governments bordering Afghanistan. These semi-autonomous areas, where the Pakistani government rarely intrudes, were likely hiding places

Box 19 Going cheap in Pakistan.

U.S. aid package promised Pakistan in 2003:

$600 million a year

= 0.2 percent of Pakistan's GDP

= 1¢ per day per person in Pakistan

of Al Qaeda leaders, as of 2003. Musharraf was our best means of getting at them. Meanwhile, Pakistan has a growing arsenal of nuclear weapons, aimed against India, which Musharraf's government has kept under control and out of the hands of America's enemies—so far. Because of Musharraf's pro-U.S. stance, Pakistani cities have been hit by terrorist bombings several times since 9/11, driving away foreign investment and hurting Pakistan's already poor economy. Musharraf himself was nearly assassinated twice in late 2003.

How much would you pay for an ally like that? Not much, it turns out. Musharraf's 2003 visit to President Bush at Camp David brought a U.S. promise of five years of economic and military aid amounting to $600 million a year, or one-fifth of 1 percent of Pakistan's GDP (see Box 19). And even that package was conditional on Pakistan's behavior and Congress's willingness to appropriate the funds, which was far from certain given the budget problems and the Iraq war costs. (In addition, but still far from sufficient, the United States wrote off $1 billion in Pakistani debts, and Western governments rescheduled $12 billion more.)

Nor did Bush grant Musharraf's request for help in resolving the Kashmir dispute with India, which had brought the nuclear-armed nations to the brink of war as recently as 2002. It is a complicated issue, which American energies and resources might help move forward. Kashmir is one of three territories—the others being Palestine and Chechnya—seen by sympathetic Muslims worldwide as representing Muslim populations ruled by non-Muslim armies of occupation. (Some would add Iraq to that list in 2003.) Because Kashmir affects the War on Terror, we need to pay more attention and put in more resources. But this competes with other international and domestic priorities, such as Iraq and tax cuts.

In September 2003, Musharraf complained that his government lacked the military equipment—especially helicopters—directly needed to pursue Al Qaeda near the Afghanistan border. "You know, you get the information [about terrorists' location] . . . Can you go on foot? They'll know that you're coming two days before you reach the place. Can you go on vehicles? There are no roads and tracks. So therefore obviously you have to have aerial mobility. Which means helicopters. Helicopters for transport of troops. Helicopter gunships for attack. O.K.? Pakistan is deficient of both. O.K.? We are trying to get both. And again, U.S. assistance is required."[8] But not forthcoming.

Then there is the matter of twenty-eight F-16 fighter jets that Pakistan bought from the United States fifteen years ago and paid for but never received. We embargoed the planes to punish Pakistan for going nuclear, and we also refused to refund the money—hundreds of millions of dollars—for fifteen years. Finally we agreed to pay it back in soybean oil and wheat, which we previously gave them for free. The payment was without interest, and we charged millions of dollars in storage fees for keeping the planes for fifteen years. Pakistani public opinion considers all this something of a slap in the face. General Musharraf pushed hard for the planes at Camp David in June 2003. "You're never going to escape this," Musharraf joked to Bush at a joint press conference where Bush announced that he would not sell F-16s to Pakistan. Give Musharraf the planes and he's a hero to his people and, equally important, to his military. The jets would help change a widespread Pakistani perception that cooperation with America's War on Terror is a one-way street.[9]

There are some arguments against selling F-16s to Pakistan, and as a practical matter it may be impossible to get Congress to agree to it. But we *could* give the money back with interest, instead of paying in "free" soybean oil that suddenly isn't— only a step above magic money. The War on Terror demands the commitment of serious resources. But to pay Pakistan's money back for real would cost the U.S. taxpayers. It would have to come at the expense of some American constituency. The proposed 2003 aid package of $600 million a year more than makes up for the F-16 money, but it is too little and too late to get us, or Musharraf, much credit with the Pakistani public.

What Pakistanis want more than F-16s or helicopters is to sell us shirts. The textile and clothing industries account for more than half of Pakistan's industrial employment and 80 percent of the country's export earnings. Labor-intensive textile production has long been a key sector for getting industrialization started in poor countries. Cotton garments are especially labor intensive and therefore provide many jobs. But the United States imposes tariffs on textiles and clothing from Pakistan, among many other quotas and tariffs that limit imports of these goods. In the winter of 2002, after Pakistan's exports dropped, tens of thousands of workers were laid off—this in an extremely poor country with few resources to fall back on.[10]

Pakistan asked the United States and European Union to lower the tariffs to help, in exchange for Pakistan's help in the War on Terror. The Europeans did so, though not fully. But the

United States did very little. In fact, at the World Trade Organization meeting in fall 2001 in Doha, Qatar, U.S. trade representative Robert Zoellick fought to preserve the current trading rules that allow rich countries to protect their textile industries. Zoellick stuck to his guns on textiles even while giving ground in other areas of negotiation, and despite efforts by developing countries to push the textile issue as a prime concern. Back in Pakistan, preachers in mosques in textile-producing cities blamed the layoffs on the United States.[11]

So why not lower the tariffs and let the Pakistanis sell us shirts? Pakistanis will be happier and more pro-American—admittedly not saying much, given the state of Pakistani public opinion toward America—and Musharraf will have a bit more political space to take actions that help us but are unpopular in Pakistan. It seems simple.

The problem is that clothing imports from Pakistan compete with U.S.-made clothing, so efforts to help Pakistani workers would hurt American workers. The U.S. textile industry employs nearly half a million Americans who, unlike Pakistanis, vote here. And the U.S. textile industry is in its worst crisis in decades, a crisis that began when the 1997 devaluation of Asian currencies made textile imports much cheaper. According to the textile industry association, more than 150,000 American textile jobs have been lost, and hundreds of mills closed, in recent years.

When the idea of lowering barriers to Pakistani textiles came up after 9/11, the president of the textile association was the late Charles Hayes, chairman of Guilford Mills of Greensboro, North Carolina. Hayes was a six-foot-four-inch, three-hundred-pound powerhouse in the industry and an experienced lobbyist "famous for button-holing congressmen, literally going toe-to-toe, nose-to-nose," as one obituary later recalled. He liked free trade for his company's and his industry's products. In fact he relocated some Guilford factories to Mexico after NAFTA, which he had supported vigorously. But imports from Pakistan were the enemy, and Charles Hayes took to the trenches after 9/11. He argued that Pakistani exporters were not actually doing that badly—that the whole thing was a setup by big greedy textile importers to profit from a flood of cheap imports, at the expense of U.S. workers. Mostly he argued that whatever needed to be done to help Pakistan should not fall unfairly on the U.S. textile industry.[12]

Victory came in December 2001 when Congress took up the fast-track bill authorizing President Bush to negotiate new trade agreements without congressional meddling. That bill was important to Bush, and to get it passed he needed the votes of a handful of Republican representatives from textile districts in North Carolina, Georgia, and Kentucky. So he met with them at the White House and promised that any actions regarding Pakistan would not hurt U.S. textile companies. The leader, Robin Hayes of North Carolina—himself a wealthy mill owner—then dropped his opposition and voted for the fast-track trade bill, which passed by one vote.

Despite some later complaints about implementation, the industry had won. As Charles Hayes said, "We are especially pleased that there will be no cuts in duties on imported textile and apparel products from Pakistan. . . . The Administration has listened to the concerns of the industry and its supporters in Congress, and has developed a balanced and acceptable package which ensures that the cost of aiding this important ally is broadly shared by all Americans, not just American textile companies and American textile workers."[13]

It makes some sense that the costs of the War on Terror should be equitably distributed and not arbitrarily piled on the hard-hit textile industry. But then who *should* bear the burden of this war? It shouldn't fall on the travel industry or the steel industry, both badly hurting. It shouldn't fall on New York, which has already suffered more than its share, nor on high-unemployment states such as Oregon. And of course it shouldn't fall on swing states in the presidential election, such as Florida and Ohio! It's a lot easier for politicians to spare all these constituencies and just cut corners on the war effort instead.

Not only did the textile industry win continued protection from imports, and President Bush win his coveted fast-track bill, but Congressman Robin Hayes went on to win reelection in 2002, after massively outspending his opponent and bringing in President Bush personally to campaign.[14] So it was win–win–win. Only a bunch of Pakistanis lost. And they don't vote here. The trouble is, a lot of them sympathize with America's enemies, and a few of them know how to make nuclear weapons. By 2003, a wildfire of anti-Americanism raged unchecked in Pakistan.

Back in November 2001, Musharraf had told Bush, according to Bob Woodward, that "his deep fear was that the United States would in the end abandon Pakistan, and that other interests would crowd out the war on terrorism." Bush reportedly answered, "Tell the Pakistani people that the president of the United States looked you in the eye and told you we wouldn't do that."[15] Right. Unless it's the only way to pass an important trade bill.

Democracy and Self-Interest

Our democracy these days is dominated by the pull and tug of self-interested groups, as I have said. Does this political style still serve us in wartime? Author Steven Brill argues that it does. In his survey of the changing American society after 9/11, Brill concludes that "what we really saw in the first year after the attacks was how resilient a system could be that is built not only on a generosity of spirit in a time of crisis but also on people asserting their selfish interests in an arena full of competitors who do the same thing. Their battles more often than not produced a messy, drawn-out, but good result." Brill points to the creation of the Department of Homeland Security as a politically difficult feat that was accomplished after much political wrangling. Brill makes the point that progress in adapting to a post-9/11 world "came amid partisan and special interest bickering—in other words . . . in an environment in which everyone assumed their usual roles." Brill celebrates America's "mix of public and private motives"—altruism and selfishness. "The results have hardly been perfect . . . [but] are far better than most would have imagined" right after 9/11.[16]

But if Brill's claim stood the test of the first year after 9/11, it surely fails the second year. The political system, as it drifted back to business as usual, did not muster the resources to move the War on Terror forward decisively. Brill's claim that "the special interest, turf-jealous system that is America ended up curing itself" would sound a lot more convincing if we had won the war or had victory in sight. Brill himself notes that "democracy under-reacts to a real threat that it should be addressing when there is not a perceived crisis to focus attention on it."[17]

In Brill's own accounts of Canadian border security, the actual results of the political tugs-of-war undermine his claim that the system worked. Before 9/11, he reports, along a section of Minnesota's border with Canada with twenty-four U.S. Customs entry points, sixteen had nothing at night but an orange traffic cone in the road and a sign telling people to come back in the morning to get inspected. Brill traces the processes by which border procedures were tightened without choking off trade. The sixteen unguarded crossing points got staffed at night, right after 9/11. "Of course," Brill says, "anyone really wanting to sneak in could still go around these official ports of entry and walk over through the woods or on a dirt road. But it was a start." Hello? "Anyone really wanting to sneak in" is who we're talking about. As Brill later notes, terrorists "had to know that it was ridiculous to try to come through an official port of entry when they could walk over any of the thousands of miles of the unguarded border, drive across many parts of it, or take a boat in over the rest."

Describing border procedures in place nine months later, after the give and take of our political process had produced a response, Brill uses the same phrase, "it was a start." Although cameras and sensors had been installed at crossings, he writes, "this didn't solve the problem of people coming over the border between official ports of entry, such as at [a] dock in Detroit, or in rural areas. . . . But it was a start." In April 2002, as Tom Ridge showed off a new cargo security system at the busy Ambassador Bridge, half a mile away "small boats [were] docking on the shores of Detroit completely unchallenged." In September 2002, Brill gave a grade of "D-" to border security a year after 9/11. "A terrorist could still move weapons of mass destruction through Canada's relatively porous borders" and then into the United States in the Great Lakes region "where the Coast Guard and Border Patrol are still almost hopelessly understaffed."[18] So how can Brill claim that our system of self-interested democracy produced a "good result"?

I come back to the need for political leadership to transcend self-interested motives and inspire us to shared sacrifice, as President Kennedy did in telling us to "ask not what your country can do for you." The point is not, as Brill has it, that the usual mix of selfishness and generosity in American politics will get us through. The point is to *change the mix,* to unleash generosity and tame selfishness, to lash the public spirit to the wagons and drag them forward to the finish line, with determination, at risk of unthinkable costs if we fail.[19]

Chapter Eleven

PAY TO WIN

How will we know when the War on Terror is over? Defense Secretary Rumsfeld was asked that question at a briefing in March 2002. First he said, "I suppose that will be something that the President would make a judgment on, as to when it was over." Then he added, "I think that the way I would characterize the end of the conflict is when we feel that there are not effective global terrorist networks functioning in the world." When asked how long the United States could maintain the war on terrorism, Rumsfeld replied, "As long as it is necessary, and let there be no doubt." Earlier, two weeks after 9/11, Rumsfeld predicted that "this is not something that . . . ends with a significant event," such as the signing of the Japanese surrender in 1945. "It is something that will involve a sustained effort over a good period of time. . . . It is by its very nature something that cannot be dealt with by some sort of massive attack or invasion."[1]

Is victory possible? My response is that we have to make sure it *is* possible. We must, in the coming few years, meet a challenge that could otherwise destroy our society in the coming decades. Defining victory, following Rumsfeld, as the elimination of global terrorist networks, I can see no reason in theory why we could not accomplish that task. Our methods will not resemble past wars. Traditional military campaigns alone cannot secure victory, although they may be necessary components of a victory. Nonmilitary methods include diplomacy, foreign aid, communications, energy policy, and other dimensions of national action toward the elimination of global terrorist networks. In my view, we should be pushing forward vigorously on *all* these dimensions, not relying unrealistically on either military or nonmilitary means alone to do the job. But whether you think military or nonmilitary aspects matter most, there is a basic relationship between the money (and other resources) we put into the effort and how quickly that effort succeeds. Right now, as the preceding chapters show, the effort is not succeeding quickly enough. So, logically, we should try putting more money into it, in addition to the adjustments we might make to the balance of military and nonmilitary means of counterterrorism. By mobilizing all our resources, sharing the sacrifice of paying for them, and focusing our collective attention on the task, we could increase our odds of winning and getting back to peace. At least we should try.

The phrase "for the duration" refers to the period until a current war ends. It has been used in many historical wars, usually referring to the terms of conscription or enlistment, but it took on a broader meaning during the world wars—total wars that pulled civilian life into the fray. The world wars engendered the widespread feeling that we were all in it together—and expected to suffer disruptions and costs in our lives—"for the duration." The concept of "the duration" would be useful to resurrect in the present war, since it implies a finite time beyond which the promise of peace beckons.

Two Timelines

The 9/11 attacks have been compared with the Japanese attack on Pearl Harbor on December 7, 1941, in terms of loss of thousands of American lives and shock to the national psyche. After Pearl Harbor, President Franklin Roosevelt made this promise: "No matter how long it may take us . . . the American people in their righteous might will win through to absolute victory."[2] Sure enough, the American people did just that. The task was much harder and the stakes much higher than anything we face today. But the country did it.

This time we can start the clock on September 11, 2001, notwithstanding some earlier skirmishes (they blew up our embassies; we cruise-missiled their training camp). Consider the progress through mid-2003, nearly two years into the war. A report by the British think tank International Institute for Strategic Studies found Al Qaeda "more insidious and just as dangerous" as before 9/11. The U.S. troops hunting for terrorists in Afghanistan suffered from too little information, too little understanding of the country, and far too few language interpreters ("terps," as the soldiers call them). Terrorists found sanctuary in Pakistan where U.S. forces could not follow, and the training of an Afghan national army had been "painfully slow," according to journalist Daniel Bergner, with fewer than five thousand soldiers trained out of seventy thousand needed. A U.S. Special Forces commander, Chris Allen, said that he had talked with village elders about building schools and clinics, which he wanted to do, but that he lacked funds for such projects. All the army reconstruction projects in Afghanistan together had just $12 million, about fifty cents per capita. A year and a half after U.S. power routed the Taliban, Bergner found Afghan children eating "bin Laden candies, sugary balls in wrappers showing the leader's face, his pointed finger and the tip of a rocket."[3]

By an equivalent date after Pearl Harbor—October 1943—the United States had turned the Pacific tide at Midway, retaken Guadalcanal, driven Axis forces from North Africa, and forced Italy's surrender. Millions of Americans—including many women for the first time—had taken new war jobs, increasing aircraft production tenfold and turning out tens of thousands of planes a year, as well as thousands of ships and hundreds of thousands of tanks and trucks. In 1943 pennies were made from steel to save copper for the war effort—reportedly enough in all for more than a million artillery shells. You knew from the money in your pocket that we were at war. Kids collected scrap metal on the streets and turned it in for use in the war effort. Actually, a lot of the recycled stuff that Roosevelt encouraged civilians to collect was not useful in the war industries. But he knew that the sense of involvement, investment, and participation that Americans would feel *was* needed for the war effort.

The whole of U.S. participation in World War II took 1,364 days from Pearl Harbor to Japan's surrender. This time, 1,364 days will bring us to June 6, 2005. On that date, will we have reached "absolute victory" and be returning to peacetime? More likely, a second-term president or a new president will be buckling down to the next phase of a long, ongoing, costly war. The difference is that last time the country fully mobilized to win. This time it has not done so.

The War on Terror has been called a new Thirty Years' War. Benjamin and Simon make the connection to the Thirty Years' War of 1618–48, in which "the ferocity of the killing . . . was

fueled by religious hatred." They think the War on Terror similarly "could take a generation to finish." This book has detailed
the many costs and risks—both physical and economic—of allowing the war to drag on in this way. The original Thirty
Years' War was a disaster for the people of central Europe. Historian Theodore Rabb writes that it was "above all . . . regarded,
ever since their own day, as one of the worst catastrophes in
history." Historian Michael Howard calls the period a "nadir of
brutality" in which "warfare seemed to escape from rational
control . . . and to degenerate instead into universal, anarchic,
and self-perpetuating violence." With the economy in ruins, especially in Germany, only mercenaries could find work, and a
soldier was "well described as a man who had to die so as to
have something to live on," writes Howard. War-induced
famine and plague killed as much as one-third of the German
population. The idea of a new Thirty Years' War holds no appeal whatsoever.[4]

Three Fronts

To avoid that prospect, we will have to do a better job of mobilizing the full energies of the country for a few years to end
the threat decisively. Better to pay now than remain "at war"
and at risk indefinitely. To prevail in years rather than decades,
we need to recognize the multiple dimensions in which this
war is fought and pour resources into all of them. Three major
"fronts" need our attention—military actions, homeland security, and foreign aid/diplomacy. These three fronts correspond
with three large federal bureaucracies—the departments of Defense, Homeland Security, and State, respectively. President
Bush speaks about all three aspects as components of the War
on Terror.

As a thought experiment, I propose that we increase spending on missions related to the War on Terror by something on the order of $100 a month per average household (raising the total from $500 to $600 a month). This new spending, about $120 billion per year "for the duration," would fund the three major "fronts" with $40 billion each. I argue that such an increase, which we can afford if we are willing to sacrifice, would substantially increase the chances of winning the war in the coming five years. These arbitrary numbers are put forward as a way to begin thinking about the scale of this endeavor, not as proposals. Using these numbers, we can ask what we could do with that amount of money.

My argument that we should increase spending does not depend on how we fight the war. If you think, "War is not the solution, I wouldn't spend a penny more on the Pentagon," you are still left with two-thirds of the increase I propose. Similarly, if you think, "I'll fight the bad guys but I'm not putting a dime into liberal do-good programs to help the needy," you are again left with two-thirds of the total to pay. However you slice it, the costs are going up in the coming years.

Military Spending

To start off, military forces have received large funding increases since 9/11. But because spending had decreased in the 1990s, the 2004 military budget still comes to just 10 percent higher than the average level for the Cold War years, adjusted for inflation. Even including the supplemental appropriations for Iraq brings it to around the level of spending (about $450 billion a year) during the Korean and Vietnam wars and the Reagan buildup. But Korea and Vietnam put a much greater strain on the U.S. economy because the economy was much smaller then. Today's level of military spending taken as a percent of GDP—less than 5 percent, and still only about 6 percent counting all war-related spending—is unusually low for wartime.

Do we need to spend as much as we do on the military? Some critics of military spending say that we would not need to spend so much on the military if we had not gone into Iraq. But we cannot rewrite history. Americans differ on whether overthrowing Saddam Hussein was a necessary action in the War on Terror or a really stupid mistake—Vietnam on fastforward. But none of that matters for our decisions today about how much to spend on the War on Terror and how to raise it. We will pay for Iraq, for better or worse, in the coming years. As President Bush put it in September 2003, "We will do what is necessary, we will spend what is necessary" in Iraq.[5] One certainty of the next presidential term, whether Bush's or not, will be the necessity to spend a great deal of money on Iraq.

Other critics point to Pentagon waste—the proverbial $600 toilet seat custom-made for an airplane—to argue that military funds are not well spent. But these "what if" questions miss the point. We cannot change the practices of a huge bureaucracy overnight, midwar. The Pentagon is what it is, and in the next five years we need it to win wars and—unlike in Afghanistan and Iraq—win decisively and finish the job. If it costs the occasional $600 per toilet seat to do that, we will pay for it.

Another criticism of current military spending is that the national missile defense program wastes billions of dollars. The program is seemingly a bottomless pit for money, perhaps on the order of $100 billion to get an initial system running. It will at best protect against only long-range ballistic missiles. While that may be a good idea—you can argue about whether it will ever work technically and whether it's worth the cost—

the money still competes with other needs more relevant to the War on Terror. According to the January 2002 National Intelligence Estimate, produced by the CIA, an attack on the United States by "ships, trucks, airplanes, or other means" is more likely than one by ballistic missiles.[6]

But the missile defense budget is far smaller than the needs of the overall War on Terror. Since the $100 billion just mentioned is spread over a decade, the missile defense bill comes to only about 2 percent of Pentagon spending—$9 billion in 2004, or about $7 a month per household. If the Pentagon needs more money to win the War on Terror, it needs that money whether or not we deploy a missile defense system. The truth is that 60 percent of Pentagon spending goes for salaries, operations, and maintenance, with only a third for research, development, and purchase of all weapons and supplies. And most of the weapons and supplies are far from high-tech (fuel, food, trucks, etc.). The $600 toilet seats and fancy missile defense radars do not make up the bulk of the defense budget.

My thought experiment would raise military spending by $40 billion—$30 per average household per month. That's about 10 percent of the current level, not counting supplemental appropriations. I will keep this figure deliberately arbitrary because its purpose is to get a sense of an order of magnitude rather than to add up any particular shopping list. Such an increase would be a significant boost to military efforts to accomplish its new tasks worldwide in the War on Terror.

Homeland Security

Homeland security is seriously underfunded. Whole areas of the homeland security budget—such as port security, first responders, and border security—need much larger infusions of money and personnel. Recall from Chapter 8 that a Council on Foreign Relations task force on emergency responders recommended *tripling* funding in that area to $20 billion a year (i.e., increasing from about $5 to $15 a month per household). Port security alone needs at least several billion dollars a year in new spending.

States and cities need a lot more help paying for the unfunded federal mandates and other new security-related costs. A Brookings Institution analysis estimated the costs of homeland security in fiscal year 2004 at $48 billion, of which around $7 billion will be paid by state and local governments. The National Conference of State Legislatures estimated that unfunded federal mandates to states in 2003 concerning homeland security totaled at least $4 billion. If state and local governments are broke, the job will not get done. For example, in 2003, Seattle wanted a new police boat to help patrol the waterfront but could not afford it. The city had already spent $6 million of its scarce funds on post-9/11 security costs such as patrolling power plants, bridges, and reservoirs and beefing up the fire department's emergency response units.[7]

To jump-start the lagging homeland security programs in local communities, my thought experiment would provide a massive infusion of federal funds to local governments and other "first providers." The $40 billion increase would basically double everything the federal government spends on homeland security, picking up local costs while simultaneously expanding federal efforts in areas such as border and port security. Before this is over, we may be equipping our commercial air fleets with antimissile technologies. We may be monitoring every dirt road across every border and sniffing the air at thousands of locations for traces of biological or chemical weapons. We might even actually give long-promised aid to local communities in full, to remedy widespread deficiencies in first-responder capabilities.

As with military spending, not all the money is well spent. The allocation of new homeland security spending remains highly political, with winners and losers resulting from a lot of horse-trading. Congressional spending on preparation for a terrorist attack came to $10.00 per person in Wyoming but only $1.40 in New York. Jamie Metzl directed a Council on Foreign Relations task force on emergency response to a terrorist attack. On *Meet the Press,* he complained that "many of the distribution formulas come from Congress and about 40 percent of the homeland security funds . . . are evenly distributed among states. And the remaining 60 percent is divided according to population. We can't have a divide-the-spoils system. . . . This is too important. What we need to do is a threat and vulnerability assessment and allocate our resources to address our most urgent needs."[8]

That's a fine thing to do, but we will not be able to delay spending money on homeland security while we fix our divide-the-spoils political system. Rather, we may need to allocate more money to make sure the job gets done despite these inefficiencies. My arbitrary funding increase of $40 billion a year, or $30 per household per month, would certainly make a huge difference in meeting our homeland security needs.

Foreign Aid and Diplomacy

The third major front, foreign aid and diplomacy, is severely underfunded. Clearly, the United States is losing ground in the vital effort to take away support from Al Qaeda and to gain allies and friends worldwide.

Of the many global battlegrounds in the War on Terror, one was a humiliating rout in 2003—the battle for public opinion in countries that are either powerful U.S. allies or that contain large populations potentially sympathetic to Al Qaeda and other anti-American groups. A Pew poll in early 2004 measured favorable opinion of Osama bin Laden at about 65 percent in Pakistan, 55 percent in Jordan, and 45 percent in Morocco. Unfavorable opinions of President Bush were held by 65 percent, 95 percent, and 90 percent of the public in the three countries, respectively—as well as by 85 percent in Germany and France, 60 percent in Britain and Russia, and 65 percent in Turkey. Each of these eight countries is traditionally a strong ally of the United States (Russia more recently than the rest), and each has an important role to play if the War on Terror is to succeed. So something has gone badly wrong.[9]

Consider Indonesia, Pakistan, Turkey, and Nigeria, which span the Muslim world. Their combined population of more than five hundred million is twice that of the United States and represents half of all the world's Muslims. These are the big fish. How do these half a billion Muslims in four countries view the United States? In particular, do they buy President Bush's assertion that the War on Terror is not directed against Islam? A poll in May 2003 asked, "How worried are you that the U.S. could become a threat to your country someday?" Respondents could choose "Not at all," "Not too much," "Somewhat," or "Very." In each of the four large Muslim countries, more than 70 percent were either somewhat worried or very worried. It wasn't any better in Russia, a critically important partner in nonproliferation—71 percent. Among Indonesians, Palestinians, and Jordanians, large majorities expressed some level of confidence in Osama bin Laden. In Indonesia, Pakistan, Turkey, and Jordan, less than a quarter of the population supported the U.S. War on Terror, and in Morocco, less than a tenth did. Whether Moroccans' opinions were changed by the multiple car bombs that killed forty-one people in Casablanca two days after the polling ended, I do not know. But clearly, the United States is losing the war for public opinion in key Muslim countries.

The poll was part of a broad survey of thirty-eight thousand people in forty-four nations conducted by the Pew Research Center for the People and the Press. It showed a dramatic drop in support for the United States from 2002 to 2003 as the Iraq war unfolded. In France, Germany, and Russia, the number holding a favorable view of the United States dropped from above 60 percent to below 45 percent. (American views of France, in turn, dropped from 80 percent positive to 60 percent negative as France opposed the U.S. military action in Iraq.) The only good news is that when asked the problem with America, very large majorities in the anti-American countries said "mostly Bush" rather than "America in general." (Over time, leaders come and go, but "America in general" remains.)[10]

Considering this anti-American sentiment, Congress has shortchanged the economic, diplomatic, and cultural tools of foreign policy that are most likely to solve the problem. All U.S. foreign aid amounts to about one-tenth of 1 percent of GDP, the lowest of the rich industrialized countries. Diplomacy—running embassies, paying our UN dues, paying salaries of international inspectors, and so on—uses even less money by far. The money spent by the U.S. government on nonmilitary aspects of international relations—foreign aid, diplomacy, and participation in international organizations and agreements—has grown since 9/11. But those budgets started out so far behind military spending that even sizable increases leave giant gaps between what we are achieving and what we will need to achieve. This means there is a backlog of neglected problems and needs around the world, and we know from

Afghanistan that neglected problems can come back to haunt us.

One neglected problem in particular must not fester indefinitely. The Israeli-Palestinian conflict more than any other issue inflames anti-Americanism and support for Islamic radicalism. An absolutely critical task in the War on Terror is to achieve the Israeli-Palestinian settlement that was close to fruition just days before President Bush took office. Whatever means the United States uses to achieve its stated goals—peace, a Palestinian state, and Israeli security—they will require far more resources and attention than President Bush gave them in his first three years.

Since this third front, foreign aid and diplomacy, receives less funding and less attention than the first two, let's think in a bit more depth about what could be accomplished with big spending increases. In a way, our current low spending on foreign aid and diplomacy offers an opportunity to accomplish large goals at affordable prices. To start with a simple example, we could triple the total U.S. government spending to prevent nuclear proliferation, as some experts propose, at a cost of just $2 per household monthly. To think bigger, the United States could take on major economic, political, or humanitarian projects for less money than an Iraq-style military campaign. These kinds of projects are on the agenda as tools in the War on Terror, so the public should be discussing what they might cost.

Global Health

To start with the global HIV/AIDS epidemic, the UN's AIDS fund needed about $10 billion urgently in 2003. Steady funding of $10 billion to $20 billion a year could decisively arrest

Box 20 AIDS spending in perspective of military spending.

Approximate costs of Iraq occupation
and reconstruction:
$75 billion per year

Funding that the UN needs to stop the worldwide
AIDS, tuberculosis, and malaria epidemics:
$10 to $20 billion per year

the spread of not only AIDS but also tuberculosis and malaria, saving tens of millions of lives in the coming years (see Box 20). But in 2003 the fund had pledges of only $5 billion over five years and was running out of cash, unable to fund half of the $750 million in projects already approved unless it found more money.[11]

Does the AIDS epidemic matter to the War on Terror? Well, for a start, it threatens to push entire regions—Africa, Asia, Russia—into chaos. Africa, one of Al Qaeda's arenas of operation, is already devastated by the disease. Russia may be next. Yes, the same Russia that has all those quasi-secure nuclear weapons and materials discussed in Chapter 8. "Failed states," societies where government control has broken down or war has become endemic—such as Afghanistan, Sudan, or Somalia—are havens and breeding grounds for terrorists. The AIDS epidemic threatens to create more of those. Plus, the epidemic is on track to kill more people this decade than both world wars combined, and America as the world's richest country may be expected to lead the effort against the disease if it also plans to lead the world in areas such as combating terrorism.

President Bush talked the talk. In March 2002 he acknowledged that "persistent poverty and oppression can lead to hopelessness and despair. And when governments fail to meet the most basic needs of their people, these failed states can become havens for terror."[12] In his 2003 State of the Union address, Bush surprised critics by pledging $15 billion to a new AIDS fund for fourteen of the hardest-hit countries. The $15 billion was over five years, but at $3 billion a year—about $2 a household per month—it would still be the biggest boost the worldwide fight against AIDS had received yet. Congress passed a bill promising the funds, and Bush signed it. But Bush's 2004 budget asked for only $2 billion, and that's what Congress appropriated. Even that money had various strings attached, including a requirement that the United States not pay more than a third of the world total. Polls showed Americans strongly supported using U.S. funds to combat AIDS in Africa, but only half of the public wanted us to do *more* than we are now.[13] (Polls have shown the public wildly overestimates what we do spend on foreign aid.) A strong majority agreed that others—Africans, drug companies, the United Nations—should do more. The European Union for its part could not agree on AIDS funding.

Economist Jeffrey Sachs, director of Columbia University's Earth Institute, proposed in July 2003 that the four hundred richest Americans should take on the issue directly. He calculated that those four hundred people, with an average income above $170 million each in 2000, had their taxes decrease from 30 percent of income in 1995 to 18 percent after the Bush tax cuts. Their tax savings totaled $7 billion a year, enough to fund most of America's share of the annual $25 billion needed to prevent eight million deaths a year from infectious diseases, according to a World Health Organization commission led by Sachs. "More money could . . . keep AIDS patients alive through retroviral therapy, help mothers survive the complications of childbirth and prevent hundreds of thousands of children from dying from malaria and vaccine-preventable diseases," Sachs wrote.[14] Of course, the richest four hundred are unlikely to contribute unless we tax them. A rich banker saved the nation in 1813 (see page 70), but that's not how it works anymore. (To its credit, the Bill and Melinda Gates Foundation has funded billions of dollars in global health initiatives in recent years.)

Sachs's total of $25 billion a year is a high-end proposal that would commit the resources to really succeed. Now assume the worst case, in which nobody else in the world lifted a finger to help. Could we do it single-handedly? Yes, at a fraction of the cost of the postwar administration of Iraq. It would cost the average U.S. household $20 a month. You can argue about whether money is better spent on Iraq, or on containing AIDS, or both. But the point is that the amounts of money are not out of this world; they are not unthinkable. This is something we could do, we could do big, and we could succeed at, even if no one else supported it. So far we have abdicated leadership and then only grudgingly come up with our share of a pot of money that is too small to accomplish the mission.

What goes for global health goes for education. Specifically, children in several Muslim countries who lack access to quality education turn to religious schools, where they are indoctrinated with jihadist ideology and hatred of America. Without question, a major impediment to the ability of poor Muslim countries like Pakistan and Indonesia to provide free, universal education to children is lack of money. The kinds of funds envisioned in my thought experiment, if well targeted, could make a major dent in the problem of the extremist religious schools.

Will Addressing Poverty Reduce Terrorism?

European Commission president Romano Prodi, in late 2001, made explicit the connection he saw between foreign aid and terrorism: "Without more aid there is a greater risk of terrorism, I am convinced of that. . . . It may not be a causal effect at the moment, and I cannot tell you the outburst from the South will be next year or in two years time, but I know that we are building a tragedy for tomorrow."[15]

Jamie Metzl of the Council on Foreign Relations similarly urged the United States in 2003 to "address the hopelessness fueled by poverty and disease. Hopelessness may not have been the proximate cause of the 9/11 attacks, but addressing it is certainly one critical, long-term element of effectively responding to it." Reversing the perception of America as a threat, in Metzl's view, requires action on a broad range of foreign policy issues including global warming, AIDS, poverty alleviation, and democratization, where U.S. resources could facilitate progress and reengage the world with America in a positive way. A former U.S. ambassador to NATO, Robert Hunter, and two coauthors wrote in 2002, "Promoting health abroad is not just a matter of 'doing good' . . . [but] a critical aspect of foreign policy and, indeed, of national security." The deteriorating health of poor people worldwide not only threatens to spread diseases to America and to hinder free travel and trade, they argue, but also "stalls economic development, fuels misery and alienation, impedes governance, and helps to breed violence and terrorism."[16]

Former counterterrorism officials Benjamin and Simon are more skeptical, however. They write, "The socioeconomic decline of much of the Arab and larger Muslim world plays an indirect role in generating the new terrorism. . . . But for the most part, the participants in jihad against the United States have not been poor." Rather, "the imagery of poverty fuels the anger of middle-class terrorists." They write that "the West . . . should certainly expand assistance programs. . . . The relief of human suffering is a duty in its own right. If, as a side effect, it reduces the pool of recruits for al-Qaeda or its successors, both gratitude and surprise will be in order."[17]

To win the war by all means necessary, we should consider increasing funds for foreign aid, diplomacy, and other nonmilitary international activities by something on the order of tens of billions of dollars a year—the same as for military and homeland security budgets. This would let the United States carry out a Jeffrey Sachs–style global health initiative and a range of other programs. Such a dramatic expansion of our global presence and the help we provide desperate societies could substantially deflate the appeal of ideologies centered on hatred of America. So let's say foreign aid and diplomacy spending will need to increase by the same number as the first two "fronts"—$40 billion a year, or $30 per household monthly.

How to Pay

Put together the increases for foreign aid, homeland security, and military operations (along with increased interest for borrowed war funds), and you have a good starting point for thinking about how much more we may find ourselves spending in order to win the war in the coming years. It is an increase on the order of magnitude of $120 billion a year—$100 per household monthly (see Box 21). Where could we get that kind of money?

First, let's put that sum in perspective. It is about 1 percent of GDP, raising total war-related spending from something like

Box 21 The bill for upgrading war-related spending,
per average household monthly.

UNITED STATES GOVERNMENT
WASHINGTON, D.C.

January 20, 2005

The Smith Household
12345 Main St.
Anytown, USA

Dear Ms. Jane Q. Smith:

Thank you for choosing our premium subscription plan for war-related services for your household. The "pay to win" plan should deliver better results than your previous plan. Your account will be charged for the components listed below.

Previous contract plan:

Peacetime plan	$350 per month
Post-9/11 upgrade	$150
Total	$500 per month

Additional services ordered

Pay to Win plan:

Defense Department	$30 per month
Homeland Security	$30
Foreign Aid / Diplomacy	$30
Interest on new war debt	$10
Total	$100 per month

New Monthly Total   **$600**

6 percent to 7 percent of GDP and representing an increase of about a fifth in such spending. It is $100 per household monthly, on top of the $500 in costs enumerated in Chapter 1 and the nongovernmental war costs discussed in Chapter 6. It's not small change, but we could pay it, especially if it were just for a few years—for the duration.

President Bush's budget proposals for fiscal year 2005 were unveiled in early 2004, just before this book went into production. He proposed to increase funding in each of the three fronts I have just discussed—7 percent more money for the military, 10 percent for homeland security, and 9 percent for foreign aid and diplomacy. But this incrementalism left only the military, which starts out so much larger, with the kind of funding increase I have been discussing. President Bush's proposed military increase is about $25 billion, to which supplemental appropriations will be added (perhaps more or perhaps less than the $87 billion for fiscal 2004). That's in the same ballpark as my suggestion above. But the president's proposed increases for homeland security and for foreign aid and diplomacy amount to less than $3 billion each—that is, less than a tenth of the increase proposed in my thought experiment. To win on the homeland security front, we need to fund the local agencies that have new demands placed on them by the war. Three billion dollars doesn't begin to cover any of that. Similarly, to carry out programs to win on the foreign aid and diplomacy front, we need big initiatives costing tens of billions of dollars, not the $3 billion increase proposed in Bush's budget. Actually, the Bush budget proposed cutting the U.S. contribution to the UNAIDS fund from $550 million to $200 million. Of course, the budget may be modified on its way through Congress. But big spending increases for homeland security and foreign aid and diplomacy are not on the agenda. They should be. We are not winning the War on Terror, as of early 2004, so incrementalism is not promising.

There are three obvious places to get $120 billion a year. First, we could rescind the Bush-era tax cuts. To get to about $120 billion a year, we would have to rescind most of the 2001 and 2003 cuts. Income taxes are the prime source of revenue and they are the first line of defense in funding war, as well as the fairest way to spread the burden of war costs among the population. For my money, higher income taxes are a key element of the solution to funding the War on Terror. There would be a risk that raising taxes again could slow the economy, reducing federal revenues. So tax increases would probably be geared to the state of the economy, implemented at times when the economy can absorb them.

Meanwhile, we have option number two—increase the debt again. If the economy is too weak to carry the burden of winning the war, going deeply into debt for a few years is not inappropriate. Financing the whole increase of $120 billion a year, however, would mean another huge jump in the federal deficit, which in 2004 was already passing $600 billion a year (on-budget).

Third, if we cannot raise enough through taxes or borrowing, we could find money by cutting elsewhere in the federal budget. But we would be hard pressed to find $120 billion of savings a year, since total nonmilitary federal programs and agencies (excluding Social Security and Medicare) spend about $750 billion a year. The federal budget could be reined in somewhat—if the political will existed—by limiting the inflation-compensating "cost of living allowances" (COLAs) that drive up entitlement spending, including Social Security. The actual course we follow will likely draw on all three sources of money to cover war costs in the coming years.

The ultimate prize is to end the war, establish a more secure world order, and be able to reduce war-related spending and reap a "peace dividend" in sustained prosperity, as we did in the 1990s. It is in the interest of the United States, as a great trading nation, to secure a peaceful international system in which global trade can flourish and poor nations can develop. The achievement of a more secure world order would be worth a great deal indeed, in terms of America's overall prospects for prosperity in the coming decades.

Conclusion

The United States had a strong sense of shared sacrifice and shared purpose after 9/11, before partisan agendas overtook it. We were willing to bear any burden in order to mobilize our society's *full* resources for the task at hand. For example, one of the first challenges in getting the country back on its feet in September 2001 was reopening the stock market. Each investor's interest was to sell fast, but a panic would harm all the investors. A lot of investors held off selling, at a cost to their own finances, as a patriotic sacrifice to keep markets stable when they reopened. Some saved their own money by selling fast, but enough people refrained from doing so to see the market through an orderly retreat rather than a panicky crash. Back then, Americans were in a mood to make sacrifices to pay the new costs of wartime and thus better secure not only their own future but their children's.

That spirit of service withered over the next two years, because of a lack of leadership. As columnist Thomas Friedman put it in December 2001, "There is a deep hunger in America post–September 11 in many people who feel this is their war in their backyard and they would like to be summoned by the president to do something more than go shopping." But that summons did not come.[18]

Bob Woodward put this question to President Bush in 2002: "I asked the President whether he and the country had done enough. . . . He had not put the country on a war footing, demanded sacrifices from large numbers of citizens, or taken what for him would be the unthinkable and draconian step of raising taxes or repealing his 2001 tax cuts." Had he done enough? Bush replied: "It's an interesting question. The answer is, if they hit us hard, the answer is no. If they don't hit us hard, the answer is, we did it right."[19]

But that's like saying that because a cancer patient didn't die yet, treatment is working. That's the wrong standard. You need to find the cancer in every hiding place and treat it aggressively or it will kill you. Until we win this war—using Donald Rumsfeld's definition of winning as putting out of action all terrorist groups of global reach—we must assume that if they don't "hit us hard" today or this year, they are preparing to do so in the future.

Not paying the bill for war is not an option. What is at stake in the War on Terror is the threat that nuclear weapons will destroy American cities. If campaigns in Afghanistan and Iraq are a guide, even *higher* spending would bring more favorable results, such as preventing looting and warlord rule. At home, too, more funds would improve homeland security as local police and fire departments take on new mandates with depleted budgets and (if military reservists have been activated) fewer personnel. Similarly, U.S. diplomacy and foreign aid could be more effective tools to defeat terrorism if more funds were available. Putting together all these kinds of spending, we are in no position to cut back the resources going into the War on

Terror. Rather, we will spend more in the coming years, especially if we aim to win quickly and not just stumble through.

Thus, we are in for a sharp increase in the real price of war. The United States needs to face up honestly to the costs of war and have a political debate about how to divide the bill. Just as investors are demanding honest accounting from corporations, so should citizens demand honest accounting from their government in paying for war. We can handle the truth.

Getting everyone to sacrifice for the war effort requires strong political leadership, the kind that unites rather than divides. It means putting the War on Terror first in our political priority list—ahead of cherished projects and ideological agendas, ahead of fast-track and tax cuts, ahead of prescription drug benefits, maybe even ahead of reelection. Bearing the burden of war will change our way of life in the coming years. But if the nation can pull together, as it did during World War II—and briefly after 9/11—the upcoming years could also offer a chance to turn adversity into positive change for the country, and to renew our sense of national purpose and unity.

NOTES

Notes to Introduction

1. Christine Clarridge and Warren King, "Emergency Drill Called 'Real-Life Scary,'" *Seattle Times,* May 13, 2003. Philip Shenon, "Terrorism Drills Showed Lack of Preparedness, Report Says," *New York Times,* December 19, 2003.

2. *Seattle Post-Intelligencer* Staff and News Services, "Boeing Layoffs May Be Ending: Condit Says 'Not Many' More Are Planned," *Seattle Post-Intelligencer,* May 29, 2003. Bryan Corliss, "Stuck in Neutral," *Everett Daily Herald,* May 5, 2003.

3. Daniel Benjamin and Steven Simon, *The Age of Sacred Terror* (New York: Random House, 2002), p. 156.

4. Kathy Routliffe, "Local Hospitals Cope with 'Plague on Paper,'" *Lincolnwood Review* [Ill.], May 15, 2003.

5. Office of the Press Secretary, the White House, "President Delivers Commencement Address at Coast Guard," transcript, May 21, 2003.

Notes to Chapter One

1. William D. Nordhaus, "Iraq: The Economic Consequences of the War," *New York Review of Books,* December 5, 2002.

2. Author's rounded estimates based on data from the U.S. federal budget, U.S. Census Bureau, Center for Defense Information, and Center for Strategic and Budgetary Assessments.

3. Friends Committee on National Legislation, War Resisters' League, Center for Defense Information.

4. U.S. Department of Justice (http://usdoj.gov/victimcompensation), "Explanation of Process for Computing Presumed Economic Loss," rev. August 27, 2002. Lisa Belkin, "Just Money," *New York Times Magazine,* December 8, 2002, pp. 92–150.

5. Daniel McGinn with Suzanne Smalley, "Now Families Face the Cost of War," *Newsweek,* April 21, 2003, p. 11.

6. Joseph B. Treaster, "Senate Passes Bill Limiting Insurers' Liability after an Attack," *New York Times,* November 20, 2002, p. A13.

Notes to Chapter Two

1. That is, war-related spending absorbs about a third of federal spending excluding Social Security and Medicare. Tax data in this chapter calculated from data of the Internal Revenue Service (IRS) Statistics of Income project (www.irs.gov).

2. Data aggregated and rounded, from IRS, "Individual Income Tax Returns, Preliminary Data, 2001: Data Release," table 1, in IRS, *Statistics of Income Bulletin*, winter 2002–3, publication 1136 (Rev. 4–2003), p. 143.

3. John Steele Gordon, *Hamilton's Blessing: The Extraordinary Life and Times of Our National Debt* (New York: Walker, 1997), pp. 75–76.

4. These historical data on tax brackets and rates are posted at www.irs.gov/pub/irs-soi/03inta.xls.

5. Thomas Paine, "Prospects on the Rubicon" [1787], in *The Writings of Thomas Paine,* vol. 2, Moncure Daniel Conway, ed. (New York: Knickerbocker Press, 1894).

6. Mia Taylor and Janita Poe, "Two Pictures of Mourning," *Atlanta Journal-Constitution,* May 25, 2003.

7. W. Elliot Brownlee, *Federal Taxation in America: A Short History* (New York: Cambridge University Press, 1996). David E. Rosenbaum, "Tax Cuts and War Have Seldom Mixed," *New York Times*, March 9, 2003, p. 13.

8. Jonathan D. Salant, "Offshore Companies Do $1 Billion in Business with U.S. Government," Associated Press, *Billings Gazette* [Mont.], May 27, 2003. Jonathan Weisman, "Late Deals Got Tax Cut Done," *Washington Post*, May 30, 2003, p. A5.

9. Editorial, "Close Unpatriotic Tax Haven Loopholes," *Berkshire Eagle* [Pittsfield, Mass.], May 28, 2003.

10. Major Garrett, "Surplus Relies on Corporate Taxes—Paid Early," www.CNN.com, August 23, 2001.

11. The source apparently is not, as often cited, former senator Everett Dirksen, according to the Dirksen Center at www.dirksencenter.org/featuresBillionHere.htm.

12. IRS, "Tax Stats," Historical Tables, table 21, "Federal Excise Taxes . . . by Type of Excise Tax, Fiscal Years 1995–2002," www.irs.gov.

13. Brian Francis, "Telephone Excise Tax," *IRS Statistics of Income Bulletin*, spring 2000, pp. 81–86.

14. Excise tax data from IRS Web site, www.irs.gov/pub/irs-soi/03ex21te.xls. Brian Francis, "Federal Excise Taxes, Including the Slow Death of Expired Taxes," *IRS Statistics of Income Bulletin*, summer 1999, p. 187.

15. Steven R. Weisman, *The Great Tax Wars: Lincoln to Wilson* (New York: Simon and Schuster, 2002).

16. Author's estimates based on data in *IRS Data Book 2002* and federal budget for FY2004.

Notes to Chapter Three

1. Office of Management and Budget, Executive Office of the President, "Overview of the President's 2005 Budget," posted at www.whitehouse.gov/omb/budget/fy2005/overview.html.

2. Jonathan Alter, "Lip Service vs. National Service," *Newsweek*, June 30, 2003, p. 29. Shavon Lynch press conference posted at www.jumpstart.org/main/Shavon.doc.

3. Office of the Press Secretary, the White House, "President Delivers State of the Union Address," transcript, January 29, 2002. Office

of the Press Secretary, the White House, "Press Briefing by Ari Fleischer and John Bridgeland, Executive Director of USA Freedom Corps," transcript, January 30, 2002.

4. Jeffrey Blackwell, "Local AmeriCorps May Fold," *Democrat and Chronicle* [Rochester, N.Y.], June 14, 2003.

5. Shavon Lynch press conference posted at www.jumpstart.org/main/Shavon.doc.

6. Dave Eggers, "Muting the Call to Service," *New York Times*, August 2, 2003, p. A23.

7. Office of the Press Secretary, the White House, "President Discusses War on Terrorism," transcript, November 8, 2001.

8. Ibid.

9. Office of the Press Secretary, the White House, "President Holds Prime-Time Press Conference," transcript, October 11, 2001.

10. Office of the Press Secretary, the White House, "President Promotes Citizen Corps for Safer Communities," transcript, April 8, 2002.

11. Dan Barry, "Citizen Corps? Hang On, New York," *New York Times*, April 9, 2003, p. B13.

12. Associated Press, "Veterans Shelter Receives Financial Boost," *Daily Hampshire Gazette* [Mass.], June 26, 2003, p. B1.

13. Elisabeth Bumiller, "Bush, to Criticism, Seeks Change in Head Start," *New York Times*, July 8, 2003, p. A3.

14. Celeste Garrett, "Patient Notifies Illinois That Chicago Hospital Has Mice," *Chicago Tribune*, June 4, 2003.

15. Bob Herbert, "Ready or Not," *New York Times*, August 25, 2003, p. A21.

16. Leighton Ku, "State Fiscal Relief Provides an Opportunity to Safeguard Medicaid Budgets," report, Center on Budget and Policy Priorities, Washington, D.C., June 4, 2003.

17. Tom Baxter and Drew Jubera, "Fiscal Belt Tightening Squeezes States," *Atlanta Journal-Constitution*, June 8, 2003. Rachel Graves, "Government Budget Cuts Take on Common Theme," *Houston Chronicle*, March 6, 2003. "Children's Warns Budget Cuts Endanger Services," *Pittsburgh Business Times*, June 12, 2003. Bob Herbert, "Sick State Budgets, Sick Kids," *New York Times*, January 9, 2004, p. A21.

18. Lilo H. Stainton, "50,000 May Lose Coverage: State Budget

Cuts Could Force Elimination of Health Care Plan," *Cherry Hill Courier Post* [N.J.], June 15, 2003.

19. Baxter and Jubera, "Fiscal Belt Tightening." Ronald Brownstein, "Lawmakers Press for Federal Bailouts," *Los Angeles Times,* November 26, 2002.

20. Nicholas D. Kristof, "Going Home, to Red Ink and Blues," *New York Times,* July 19, 2003, p. A27.

21. Timothy Egan, "States, Facing Budget Shortfalls, Cut the Major and the Mundane," *New York Times,* April 21, 2003, p. A1. Baxter and Jubera, "Fiscal Belt Tightening."

22. Jason Mazzone, "What Congress Owes New York," *New York Times,* April 24, 2003, p. A31.

23. Dale Russakoff, "States Use Gimmicks to Tackle Deficits," *Washington Post,* June 1, 2003, p. A1.

24. Rick Klein, "U.S. Budget Has Windfall for Mass.," *Boston Globe,* May 24, 2003, p. A1. Associated Press, "Bush Wants to Stash $1 Billion Windfall from Washington," *Naples Daily News,* June 1, 2003.

25. Barney Gimbel, "The Sound of Sirens," *Newsweek,* June 23, 2003, p. 14.

26. Philip Shenon, "Counterterror Aid Is Tied Up by the States, Mayors Assert," *New York Times,* September 18, 2003. Charles Pope, "War on Terrorism: Security Costs Weigh Heavily at Local Level," *Seattle Post-Intelligencer,* February 10, 2003. "Cities, States Quarrel over Security Costs," Associated Press, April 7, 2003.

27. Graves, "Government Budget Cuts," p. 54.

28. Dean E. Murphy, "Down and Out, Golden Gate Is Planning to Pass the Hat," *New York Times,* November 29, 2002, p. A1. Sunshine Dewitt, "Fare Hike: PVTA Riders Bear Budget Burden," *Daily Hampshire Gazette* [Mass.], June 12, 2003.

29. Kathy A. Gambrell, "Making the Grade: No Child Left Behind," United Press International, June 11, 2003.

30. Baxter and Jubera, "Fiscal Belt Tightening." Abby Goodnough, "Teachers Dig Deeper to Fill Gap in Supplies," *New York Times,* September 21, 2002, p. A1.]

31. Philip Shenon, "Two Studies Cite Confusion on Terrorism," *New York Times,* August 21, 2003, p. A14.

32. Houston Independent School District, "Parents: Letter from Superintendent of Schools Dr. Kaye Stripling," March 17, 2003.

Notes to Chapter Four

1. Alex Berenson, "The Deficit Is Big, but Is It Bad?" *New York Times,* July 20, 2003, p. WK3.

2. Concord Coalition, "We Ask Our Soldiers to Sacrifice; What about the Rest of Us?" advertisement, *New York Times,* October 13, 2002, p. WK14. Concord Coalition, "The Truth about Entitlements and the Budget," press release, March 10, 2003. Concord Coalition, "Concord Coalition Warns That the New 'Surplus' Is Not New Money, It's Simply a New Projection," press release, June 26, 2000.

3. John Steele Gordon, *Hamilton's Blessing: The Extraordinary Life and Times of Our National Debt* (New York: Walker, 1997), p. 6.

4. United Nations, *World Economic and Social Survey 2001* (New York: United Nations, 2001), pp. 279–83, based on IMF, OECD, and World Bank data.

5. Martin Muhleisen and Christopher M. Towe, eds., "U.S. Fiscal Policies and Priorities for Long-Run Sustainability," International Monetary Fund Occasional Paper No. 227, January 7, 2004.

6. Alice M. Rivlin and Isabel V. Sawhill, *Restoring Fiscal Sanity: How to Balance the Budget* (Washington, D.C.: Brookings Institution, 2004).

7. Jeff Madrick, "The Iraqi Time Bomb," *New York Times Magazine,* April 6, 2003, pp. 48–51.

8. Niall Ferguson, "True Cost of Hegemony: Huge Debt," *New York Times,* April 20, 2003, p. WK1.

9. Daniel Altman, "First, the War; Now, Investor Consequences," *New York Times,* April 30, 2003, p. C1.

10. On-budget deficit (not reduced by amount of Social Security surplus). Interest is gross interest on U.S. Treasury debt, including interest paid to trust funds. Source: U.S. budget, FY2004.

11. Kilolo Kijakazi and Robert Greenstein, "What the Trustees' Report Indicates about the Financial Status of Social Security," report, Center on Budget and Policy Priorities, Washington, D.C., March 17, 2003. Robert Dodge, "Medicare Could Be Broke by 2019," *Dallas*

Morning News, March 24, 2004. Eric Black, "Deficit Is a Ticking Time Bomb," *Star Tribune* [Minneapolis/St. Paul, Minn.], June 17, 2003.

12. John Maynard Keynes, "A Tract on Monetary Reform" [1923], in *The Collected Works of John Maynard Keynes,* vol. 4, Donald Moggridge, ed. (London: Macmillan, 1971), p. 65.

13. Sun Tzu, *The Art of War,* trans. Samuel B. Griffith (Oxford: Oxford University Press, 1963), p. 63.

14. Ibid., p. 72.

15. Michael Howard, *War in European History* (Oxford: Oxford University Press, 1976), p. 27. Fernand Braudel, *The Perspective of the World* (New York: Harper and Row, 1984), p. 61. Fernand Braudel, *The Mediterranean and the Mediterranean World in the Age of Philip II* [1949] (repr., London: Collins, 1972), p. 1221. See also pp. 943, 1134, and 1218.

16. Sun Tzu, *Art of War,* p. 73.

17. Gordon, *Hamilton's Blessing,* pp. 42–45.

18. Ibid., pp. 45–49.

19. Ibid., pp. 49–52.

20. Ibid., p. 53.

21. Ibid., pp. 67–89. Office of Management and Budget, *The Budget for Fiscal Year 2004: Historical Tables* (Washington, D.C.), table 7.1, pp. 116–17.

Notes to Chapter Five

1. Sun Tzu, *The Art of War,* trans. Samuel B. Griffith (Oxford: Oxford University Press, 1963), p. 74.

2. Earl J. Hamilton, "The Role of War in Modern Inflation," *Journal of Economic History* 37, no. 1 (1977): 17–18. Joshua S. Goldstein, *Long Cycles: Prosperity and War in the Modern Age* (New Haven: Yale University Press, 1988).

3. I thank Professor Gerald Bender for this report.

4. Carroll Quigley, *Tragedy and Hope: A History of the World in Our Time* (New York: Macmillan, 1966), p. 256. Hamilton, "Role of War."

5. Jean de Bloch [Ivan Stanislavovich Bloch], *The Future of War in Its Technical, Economic, and Political Relations: Is War Now Impossi-*

ble? (Boston: Ginn and Company, 1899). Norman Angell, *The Great Illusion* (London: William Heinemann, 1910).

6. John Steele Gordon, *Hamilton's Blessing: The Extraordinary Life and Times of Our National Debt* (New York: Walker, 1997), pp. 73–74. Roger L. Ransom, "Economics of the Civil War," in EH.Net Encyclopedia, edited by Robert Whaples, August 25, 2001, http://www.eh.net/encyclopedia/ransom.civil.war.us.php.

7. Data are from U.S. Census Bureau Web site, www.census.gov/hhes/income/income01/cpiurs.html.

8. David Leonhardt, "Greenspan, Broadly Positive, Spells Out Deflation Worries," *New York Times*, May 22, 2003, p. C1. Paul Krugman, "Fear of a Quagmire?" *New York Times*, May 24, 2003, p. A29. Robert J. Samuelson, "Deflation Bogeyman," *Washington Post*, May 14, 2003.

9. Mike Meyers, "Deflation Not a Concern to Many Economists," *Star Tribune* [Minneapolis/St. Paul, Minn.], May 14, 2003.

10. Paul Krugman, "A Fiscal Train Wreck," *New York Times*, March 11, 2003, p. A29.

11. David E. Rosenbaum, "Greenspan Says Tax Cut without Spending Reductions Could Be Damaging," *New York Times*, May 1, 2003, p. A29. Edmund L. Andrews, "To Trim Deficit, Greenspan Urges Social Security and Medicare Cuts," *New York Times*, February 26, 2004, p. A1.

12. David Leonhardt, "As Companies Reduce Costs, Pay Is Falling Top to Bottom," *New York Times*, April 26, 2003, p. B1.

13. Krugman, "Fiscal Train Wreck."

14. Clyde V. Prestowitz Jr., "The Unmighty Dollar," *Newsweek*, March 24, 2003, p. 32.

Notes to Chapter Six

1. Carnegie Endowment for International Peace, *The Cost of War*, Memoranda Series, no. 2 (Washington, D.C.: Carnegie Endowment, 1940). Angus Maddison, *Phases of Capitalist Development* (New York: Oxford University Press, 1982). Carroll Quigley, *Tragedy and Hope: A History of the World in Our Time* (New York: Macmillan, 1966), pp. 256, 261.

2. Joshua S. Goldstein, *War and Gender: How Gender Shapes the*

War System and Vice Versa (Cambridge: Cambridge University Press, 2001), pp. 384–96.

3. Terry Pristin, "Different Cities, Different Security for Buildings," *New York Times,* July 9, 2003, p. C6.

4. Colin L. Powell, "An Open Letter from U.S. Secretary of State Colin L. Powell," advertisement in the *Wall Street Journal* and elsewhere, November 14, 2002. See also www.ds-osac.org.

5. Joe Sharkey, "In a Post-9/11 World, Corporate Travel Is All Business," *New York Times,* August 12, 2003.

6. "Egypt Braces for a Serious Blow to Tourism," *New York Times,* March 21, 2003, p. W1. Frank Bruni, "Travelers Are Scarce in Turkey, and So Is Business," *New York Times,* April 15, 2003, p. A8. David Barboza, "A Big Threat to Asia's Export-Driven Economies," *New York Times,* March 21, 2003, p. W1.

7. Nick Madigan, "$9.6 Billion Plan for Los Angeles Airport," *New York Times,* July 10, 2003, p. A18.

8. Based on data of Office of Travel and Tourism Industries, revised forecast, October 21, 2003, and Travel Industry Association of America Web site, www.tia.org.

9. Rachel L. Swarns, "Travel Industry Fears New Rules Could Deter Visits to the U.S.," *New York Times,* July 2, 2003, p. A2.

10. Data from Greater New York Hospital Association, *New York Times,* March 23, 2003, p. B14.

11. Bill Goldstein, "War Would Upend Plans of Publishers and Retailers," *New York Times,* March 10, 2003, p. C7. Stuart Elliott, "Threat of War Already Curbs the Budgets of Marketers," *New York Times,* March 10, 2003, p. C1.

12. Stuart Elliott, "Advertising," *New York Times,* April 2, 2003, p. C5.

13. Elizabeth Olson, "Imported Rugs Caught Up in Antiterror Rule," *New York Times,* July 26, 2003, p. B1.

14. Fareed Zakaria, "Time to Save 'Just in Time,'" *Newsweek,* November 12, 2001.

15. Maggie Myers, "Secretary Ridge Announces Container Security Initiative's Phase II," *Customs and Border Protection Today,* September 2003. I have calculated 300 inspectors x 40 hours x 60 minutes / 135,000 containers = 5.3 minutes/container.

16. Bob Davis and Greg Jaffe, "War Spending Won't Outweigh Its

Negative Impact on Economy," *Wall Street Journal,* February 4, 2003. Editorial, "The Economic Fog of War," *Wall Street Journal,* February 12, 2003.

17. Gene Marcial, "A Test of Wills on Wall Street," *Business Week,* October 29, 2002.

18. Alan Greenspan, "The Economic Outlook," testimony and question-and-answer before the Joint Economic Committee, U.S. Congress, November 13, 2002.

19. William D. Nordhaus, "The Economic Consequences of War," in *War with Iraq: Costs, Consequences, and Alternatives* (Cambridge, Mass.: American Academy of Arts and Sciences, 2002).

20. Bob Davis, "Iraq Attack Could Cost $200 Billion," *Wall Street Journal,* September 16, 2002.

21. Alex Berenson, "Learning the Economics of This War," *New York Times,* March 23, 2003, p. WK2.

22. Alan Greenspan, testimony before the Committee on Banking, Housing, and Urban Affairs, U.S. Senate, February 11, 2003.

23. Barbara Hagenbaugh, "War Could Fix or Flatten Economy," *USA Today,* February 4, 2003.

24. Steve Lohr, "The War Goes Well. So Where's the Dividend?" *New York Times,* April 13, 2003, p. BU1. Robert J. Samuelson, "Victory Is No Panacea," *Newsweek,* April 21, 2003, p. 51.

25. Daniel Altman, "First, the War; Now, Investor Consequences," *New York Times,* April 30, 2003, p. C1.

26. United Nations, *World Economic and Social Survey 2003* (New York: United Nations, 2003).

27. Steven Kull et al., "Americans on Terrorism: Two Years after 9/11," report, Program on International Policy Attitudes (PIPA), Washington, D.C., September 9, 2003.

28. N. R. Kleinfield and Marjorie Connelly, "9/11 Still Strains New York Psyche," *New York Times,* September 8, 2003, p. A17.

29. John Tierney, "The Duct Tape Jokes Are Persistent; So Is Ridge," *New York Times,* March 17, 2003.

30. Philip G. Zimbardo, "The Political Psychology of Terrorist Alarms," March 1, 2003, as posted at www.zimbardo.com.

Notes to Chapter Seven

1. Associated Press, "Success of Tomahawk Cruise Missiles Bodes Well for Lexington Company," *Daily Hampshire Gazette* [Mass.], March 26, 2003, p. B6.

2. Bob Davis and Greg Jaffe, "War Spending Won't Outweigh Its Negative Impact on Economy," *Wall Street Journal,* February 4, 2003.

3. Alan Cowell, "War a Boon for Outfitters and Trainers," *New York Times,* March 25, 2003, p. W1.

4. Bob Herbert, "What Is It Good For?" *New York Times,* April 21, 2003, p. A25.

5. Michael Dobbs, "Halliburton's Deals Greater Than Thought," *Washington Post,* August 28, 2003, p. A1. Stock history: Yahoo Financial.

6. Bernard Simon, "Trade Concerns as Canada Sits Out War," *New York Times,* April 2, 2003, p. W1.

7. Liz Ruskin, "Spending Bill Helps Alaska Salmon," *Anchorage Daily News,* April 15, 2003. James Kuhnhenn, "Despite Talk of Frugality, Spending Goes On Unabated," Knight Ridder Newspapers, June 3, 2002.

8. As posted at www.internationalanswer.org.

9. Michael Moran and Alex Johnson, "Oil after Saddam: All Bets Are In," MSNBC, November 7, 2002, posted at www.msnbc.com.

10. Ibid.

11. Donna Rosato, "War: What (Stocks) Is It Good For?" *New York Times,* November 24, 2002, p. 6.

12. Lolita C. Baldor, "Sick Veteran Battles Bureaucracy Back Home," Associated Press, August 11, 2003. Athena Desai, "Iraq Veteran Comes Home—Finds Little Help," WBUR radio, Boston, August 13, 2003.

13. Veterans of Foreign Wars, "VFW Outraged at Inadequate Funding for Veterans Health Care," press release, July 17, 2003.

14. Jonathan Turley, "Full Metal Jacket," *Los Angeles Times,* September 29, 2003.

15. Steven Greenhouse, "Balancing Their Duty to Family and Nation," *New York Times,* June 22, 2003, p. A12.

Notes to Chapter Eight

1. Daniel Benjamin and Steven Simon, *The Age of Sacred Terror* (New York: Random House, 2002), pp. 399, 418.

2. George W. Bush, introduction to *The National Security Strategy of the United States of America* (Washington, D.C.: The White House, September 17, 2002).

3. David Albright and Holly Higgins, "A Bomb for the Ummah," *Bulletin of the Atomic Scientists*, March/April 2003, pp. 49–55.

4. Thalia Assuras, "Nuclear Sentries," CBSNews.com, March 4, 2002. Bob Woodward, *Bush at War* (New York: Simon and Schuster, 2002), pp. 270–71.

5. Massimo Calabresi and Romesh Ratnesar, "Can We Stop the Next Attack?" *Time*, March 11, 2002. Sam Nunn, remarks at Carnegie Endowment for International Peace international nonproliferation conference, Washington, D.C., November 14, 2002.

6. Benjamin and Simon, *Age of Sacred Terror*, p. 205.

7. David E. Sanger, "North Korea's Bomb: Untested but Ready, C.I.A. Concludes," *New York Times*, November 9, 2003, p. 4.

8. Mohamed El Baradei, "Implementation of the NPT Safeguards Agreement in the Islamic Republic of Iran," report to the Board of Governors (Vienna: International Atomic Energy Agency, February 24, 2004).

9. Institute for Energy and Environmental Research and Physicians for Social Responsibility, "Fissile Material Basics," factsheet, March 20, 1996. Posted at http://www.ieer.org/fctsheet/fm_basic.html.

10. Dan Stober, "No Experience Necessary," *Bulletin of the Atomic Scientists*, March/April 2003, pp. 57–63.

11. Benjamin and Simon, *Age of Sacred Terror*, pp. 128–29, 147.

12. Stober, "No Experience Necessary."

13. Matthew Bunn, Anthony Wier, and John P. Holdren, *Controlling Nuclear Warheads and Materials: A Report Card and Action Plan* (Cambridge, Mass.: John F. Kennedy School of Government, Harvard University, March 2003).

14. Center for Strategic and International Studies (CSIS), "Global Partnership Update," report, Washington, D.C., November 19, 2003.

15. George W. Bush, State of the Union address, January 28, 2003. Robert Stacy McCain, "Al Qaeda Eyed for Russian Nukes," *Washington Times*, March 4, 2002.

16. Patrick Lenain, Marcos Bonturi, and Vincent Koen, "The Economic Consequences of Terrorism," Organization for Economic Cooperation and Development (OECD), Economics Department Working Papers No. 334, July 17, 2002.

17. Bunn, Wier, and Holdren, *Controlling Nuclear Warheads.*

18. Benjamin and Simon, *Age of Sacred Terror,* p. 139.

19. Diana Dean, "Prepared Statement," testimony before the Judiciary Committee, U.S. Senate, February 10, 2000.

20. David A. Lieb with Renee Ruble et al., "Terror Alerts Stretching Resources Thin," Associated Press, May 22, 2003.

21. David Chanen, "Rolling 30s Member Shot at Minneapolis Gas Station," *Star Tribune* [Minneapolis/St. Paul, Minn.], June 7, 2003.

22. Federal Emergency Management Agency (FEMA) and National Fire Protection Association (NFPA), *A Needs Assessment of the U.S. Fire Service,* FA–240, December 2002. "A Heavy Burden, Likely to Increase," *New York Times*, March 23, 2003, p. B14. Carol O'Cleireacain and Anne Nelson, "A Five-Alarm Crisis," *New York Times,* April 24, 2003, p. A31. John Nicholson, "Fire Service and Homeland Security," *NFPA Journal,* March/April 2003.

23. Warren B. Rudman, Richard A. Clarke, and Jamie F. Metzl, *Emergency Responders: Drastically Underfunded, Dangerously Unprepared,* report (New York: Council on Foreign Relations, 2003). NBC News, *Meet the Press,* transcript, June 29, 2003.

24. Tom LaTourrette et al., *Protecting Emergency Responders,* vol. 2 (Santa Monica: RAND, 2003), pp. 62, xxi.

25. Leah Samuel, "Emergency Plan Eludes City Officials," *Chicago Reporter,* February 2002. NBC5 [Chicago], "Firefighters Union Reaches Tentative Contract Agreement," March 19, 2003. NBC5 [Chicago], "Banker Donates Life-Saving Cameras to Fire Department," May 27, 2003.

26. Calabresi and Ratnesar, "Can We Stop."

27. Bunn, Wier, and Holdren, *Controlling Nuclear Warheads.*

28. Barton Gellman and Susan Schmidt, "Shadow Government Is at Work in Secret," *Washington Post,* March 1, 2002, p. A1.

Notes to Chapter Nine

1. Office of the Press Secretary, the White House, "Address to a Joint Session of Congress and the American People," transcript, September 20, 2001.

2. Bob Woodward, *Bush at War* (New York: Simon and Schuster, 2002), pp. 106, 170, 172.

3. Daniel Bergner, "Where the Enemy Is Everywhere and Nowhere" *New York Times Magazine,* July 20, 2003, pp. 38–44. Woodward, *Bush at War,* p. 315. Rod Nordland, Sami Yousafzai, and Babak Dehghanpisheh, "How Al Qaeda Slipped Away," *Newsweek,* August 19, 2002, pp. 34–41.

4. Nicholas D. Kristof, "The War on Terror Flounders," *New York Times,* May 10, 2002.

5. U.S. Department of Defense, "DOD News Briefing—Secretary Rumsfeld and General Myers," news transcript, March 28, 2002.

6. Thom Shanker, "NATO Agrees to Widen Role in Afghanistan beyond Kabul," *New York Times,* October 8, 2003, p. A10. Christopher Marquis, "General Urges NATO to Send Afghanistan More Troops," *New York Times,* January 28, 2004. Eric Schmitt, "General Urges Foreigners to Aid Afghans," *New York Times,* July 9, 2003, p. A3.

7. "Public Supports Expanding Afghanistan UN Peacekeeping Force beyond Kabul," report, Program on International Policy Attitudes (PIPA), Washington, D.C., July 8, 2003.

8. Thomas L. Friedman, "Fighting the Big One," *New York Times,* August 24, 2003, p. 11. John F. Burns, "U.S. Considers an Increase in Pay for Iraq's New Soldiers after Many Recruits Desert," *New York Times,* December 14, 2003, p. 23.

9. Editorial, "Nothing but Lip Service," *Army Times,* July 2, 2003.

10. Raymond Bonner, "U.S. Can't Locate Missiles Once Held in Iraq Arsenal," *New York Times,* October 8, 2003.

11. Peggy Noonan, *A Heart, a Cross, and a Flag: America Today* (New York: Free Press, 2003).

12. Laura Blumenfeld, "Former Aide Takes Aim at War on Terror," *Washington Post,* June 16, 2003, p. A1. Karen DeYoung and Peter Slevin, "Counterterror Team's Turnover Continues," *Washington Post,* March 20, 2003.

13. Blumenfeld, "Former Aide." Office of the Press Secretary, the

White House, "Statement on Appointment of Rand Beers as Special Assistant to the President and Senior Director for Combating Terrorism," press statement, August 15, 2002.

14. Blumenfeld, "Former Aide."

15. ABC News, *Nightline,* transcript, June 25, 2003.

16. Blumenfeld, "Former Aide."

17. Robert Novak, "Bush's Enemy Within," syndicated column, CNN.com, July 10, 2003.

18. Daniel Benjamin and Steven Simon, *The Age of Sacred Terror* (New York: Random House, 2002), p. 335.

19. Thomas E. Ricks, "Downing Resigns as Bush Aide," *Washington Post,* June 28, 2002, p. A1.

20. Eric Lichtblau, "F.B.I.'s Counterterrorism Chief Is Leaving after Three Months," *New York Times,* October 9, 2003, p. A25.

Notes to Chapter Ten

1. Democratic caucus, Appropriations Committee, U.S. House of Representatives, "The Bush Credibility Gap: February 28th Homeland Security Speech," fact sheet posted at www.house.gov/appropriations_democrats/bushdhs.pdf, March 2003.

2. John F. Kennedy, inaugural address, Washington, D.C., January 20, 1961.

3. Ronald Brownstein, "Bush Breaks with 140 Years of History in Plan for Wartime Tax Cut," *Los Angeles Times,* January 13, 2003.

4. David Firestone, "How the President's $726 Billion Plan Was Cut in Half," *New York Times,* March 26, 2003, p. A12.

5. Will Lester, "AP Poll Finds Majority of Americans Oppose Tax Cuts," Associated Press, *Fresno Bee,* April 14, 2003. The quote is from *National Journal*'s Congress Daily PM, March 12, 2003, cited by Representative George Miller, *Congressional Record,* March 12, 2003.

6. Woodrow Wilson, State of the Union address, U.S. Congress, December 7, 1915.

7. Susan Sachs, "Bush vs. bin Laden (and Other Popularity Contests)," *New York Times,* March 21, 2004, p. WK2. Data from Pew Global Attitudes Project. Bob Woodward, *Bush at War* (New York: Simon and Schuster, 2002), p. 82.

8. Felicity Barringer, "Little Chance of Pakistani Troops in Iraq," *New York Times,* September 22, 2003, p. A3.

9. Office of the Press Secretary, the White House, "President Bush Welcomes President Musharraf to Camp David," transcript, June 24, 2003. New Zealand Press Association, "Labour's Rejected Jets Flying in US," *New Zealand Herald,* July 11, 2003. Indo-Asian News Service, "US Returns Instalment for F-16s to Pakistan," *New India News,* June 22, 2003. Asian News International, "Pak to Make Fresh Payments for F-16s," *Times of India,* June 21, 2003.

10. Lael Brainard, "Textiles and Terrorism," *New York Times,* December 27, 2001.

11. Ibid. Keith Bradsher, "Pakistanis Fume as Clothing Sales to U.S. Tumble, *New York Times,* June 23, 2002.

12. Don Hogsett, "Hayes: A Powerful Legacy," *Home Textiles Today,* July 29, 2002. American Textile Manufacturers Institute (ATMI), "ATMI Opposes Proposal to Cut Duties on Pakistani Imports," news release, Washington, D.C., November 2, 2001. Charles A. Hayes, "Textiles and Terrorism—the Facts," posted on ATMI Web site, www.atmi.org, December 2001.

13. "Bush Meets with Textile Members; Says Promises Will Be Kept," *Inside U.S. Trade,* December 14, 2001, posted at ATMI Web site. American Textile Manufacturer Institute, "ATMI Reiterates Support for Administration Efforts to Combat Terrorism," news release, Washington, D.C., January 3, 2002.

14. David Perlmutt, "Hayes Holds onto Seat after Hostile Campaign," *Charlotte Observer,* November 6, 2002.

15. Woodward, *Bush at War,* p. 303.

16. Steven Brill, *After: How America Confronted the September 12 Era* (New York: Simon and Schuster, 2003), pp. 617–19, 622.

17. Brill, *After,* p. 617.

18. Brill, *After,* pp. 3, 16, 150, 420, 509. Steven Brill, "On Guard, a Year Later," *Newsweek,* September 16, 2002, pp. 38–41.

19. David Broder, "A Lump of Coal from the President," *Washington Post,* December 4, 2002. Jamie F. Metzl, "U.S. Should Recapture Spirit Spawned by 9/11," *Newsday,* April 18, 2003. Senator John McCain, "Do the Nation a Service," *Newsweek,* September 15, 2003, p. 55.

Notes to Chapter Eleven

1. U.S. Department of Defense, "DOD News Briefing—Secretary Rumsfeld and General Myers," news transcript, March 28, 2002. U.S. Department of Defense, "DOD News Briefing—Secretary Rumsfeld," news transcript, September 25, 2001.

2. Franklin D. Roosevelt, address to the nation, December 8, 1941.

3. Daniel Bergner, "Where the Enemy Is Everywhere and Nowhere," *New York Times Magazine,* July 20, 2003, p. 43.

4. Daniel Benjamin and Steven Simon, *The Age of Sacred Terror* (New York: Random House, 2002), pp. 419–20. Theodore K. Rabb, ed., *The Thirty Years' War* (New York: University Press of America, 1981), p. x. Michael Howard, *War in European History* (Oxford: Oxford University Press, 1976), p. 37.

5. Office of the Press Secretary, the White House, "President Addresses the Nation," transcript, September 7, 2003.

6. National Intelligence Council, Central Intelligence Agency, "Foreign Missile Developments and the Ballistic Missile Threat to the United States through 2015," unclassified summary, January 9, 2002. Walter Pincus, "U.S. Alters Estimate of Threats," *Washington Post,* January 11, 2002, p. A1.

7. Charles Pope, "War on Terrorism: Security Costs Weigh Heavily at Local Level," *Seattle Post-Intelligencer,* February 10, 2003.

8. NBC News, *Meet the Press,* transcript, June 29, 2003.

9. Susan Sachs, "Bush vs. bin Laden (and Other Popularity Contests)," *New York Times,* March 21, 2004, p. WK2. Data from Pew Global Attitudes Project.

10. Adam Clymer, "World Survey Says Negative Views of U.S. Are Rising," *New York Times,* December 5, 2002, p. A11. Marjorie Connelly, "Sinking Views of the United States," *New York Times,* March 23, 2003, p. WK4. Richard Bernstein, "Foreign Views of U.S. Darken after Sept. 11," *New York Times,* September 11, 2003, p. A1. See also "European View of the United States," *New York Times,* November 16, 2003, p. 15.

11. John Tagliabue, "Global AIDS Fund Finding Few Answers to Its Cash Shortage," *New York Times,* July 17, 2003, p. A4. Sheryl Gay Stolberg, "House Wrangles over Levels of Global Spending on AIDS," *New York Times,* July 24, 2003, p. A6. Joint United Nations Program

on HIV/AIDS (UNAIDS), World Health Organizations (WHO), and United Nations Children's Fund (UNICEF), "We Can Beat AIDS, TB, and Malaria, UN Agencies Say," press release, New York, April 22, 2002.

12. Office of the Press Secretary, the White House, "President Proposes $5 Billion Plan to Help Developing Nations," transcript of remarks at the Inter-American Development Bank, Washington, D.C., March 14, 2002.

13. Elizabeth Becker, "Bush Scaling Back Dollars for Third World," *New York Times*, January 29, 2004, p. A15. "Comprehensive Review of Polling on Africa Reveals Strong Support for U.S. Engagement with Africa," report, Program on International Policy Attitudes (PIPA), Washington, D.C., July 8, 2003. See also PIPA's Africa report posted at http://www.americans-world.org/digest/regional_issues/africa/africa5.cfm.

14. Jeffrey D. Sachs, "A Rich Nation, a Poor Continent," *New York Times*, July 9, 2003, p. A23.

15. Alan Friedman, "Prodi Urges More Aid to Bridge North-South Global Divide," *International Herald Tribune*, December 3, 2001.

16. Jamie F. Metzl, "U.S. Should Recapture Spirit Spawned by 9/11," *Newsday*, April 18, 2003. Robert E. Hunter, C. Ross Anthony, and Nicole Lurie, "Make World Health the New Marshall Plan," *Rand Review*, summer 2002.

17. Benjamin and Simon, *Age of Sacred Terror*, p. 409.

18. Thomas L. Friedman, "Ask Not What . . . ," *New York Times*, December 9, 2001.

19. Bob Woodward, *Bush at War* (New York: Simon and Schuster, 2002), p. 337.

ACKNOWLEDGMENTS

For her patient guidance, I thank my literary agent, Fredrica S. Friedman. For bringing the book to fruition, I thank my editor at NYU Press, Eric Zinner. This book benefited from seminars at the Program on International Politics, Economics, and Security of the University of Chicago and at the Yale political science department, and from my affiliation with the Watson Institute for International Studies at Brown University. For their ideas and suggestions, thanks to Neta Crawford, Bruce Russett, Charles Lipson, Paul Solman, George Gibson, Cal Morgan, Timothy Bartlett, John Tryneski, anonymous reviewers, Eddy Goldberg, Michael Goldstein, Joyce Galaski, John Spurr, and Christina Carpenter. On a personal note, I thank my family, friends, and Stephen Kucinski, whose hayfields I appreciate.

INDEX

ABOUT THE AUTHOR

Professor Joshua S. Goldstein, a leading expert on war and an interdisciplinary social scientist, is an associate of the Watson Institute for International Studies at Brown University. His books include *War and Gender: How Gender Shapes the War System and Vice Versa* and the top-selling undergraduate textbook *International Relations*. His work has appeared in such venues as the *New York Times,* the *Christian Science Monitor,* and the *Journal of Conflict Resolution,* and he has made numerous media appearances. For further information, please visit www.joshuagoldstein.com.